I Only Tell the Truth

Sometimes the truth doesn't shout, it whispers

Veronica Alonso

I Only Tell the Truth

Sometimes the truth doesn't shout, it whispers

Veronica Alonso

CCE PUBLISHING
Edgewater, Florida, USA

Published by
CCE PUBLISHING
Edgewater, Florida
ccepublishing.com
cindycaseyediting@gmail.com

Printed in the United States of America
ISBN Paperback: 979-8-218-82240-8
ISBN Spanish: 979-8-218-77106-5:

Dedication

To the most beautiful sky-colored eyes I've ever seen...
for being inspiration, love, serenity and joy.
Thank you for transforming my life!

Sometimes we don't need more information.
Sometimes we just need a space that reminds us of who we are when we're not afraid, or angry, or sad, or distressed.
A place where someone sees us and says:
"What you are looking for ... already lives within you." That's why I wrote this book of consciousness.
It's not just another piece of advice.
It's not motivation.
It's not a magic thought.
It's a reminder of what really matters.
That thing you already know deep down ... but often forget.

— Veronica Alonso

Table of Contents

I Only Tell the Truth

Who I Am

I don't choose the definitions, titles, or mentions. However, it's up to me to tell you who I am, and this is the way I choose to do it.

My constant vital energy has allowed me to dedicate myself to activities that have fascinated me over the years. The sensuality of movement through dance, the transformation of pain through writing, the strengthening of self-esteem and self-confidence through acting, and the unveiling of psychic depths through the analysis of my patients – and my own – exploring the symptomatic effects of emotions on the body.

I have not been one of those people who define themselves as forward-thinking. My strategy in life has been to respond to the opportunities that presented themselves at every step. Instead of planning, I've been guided more by my heart and intuition, experiencing a deep satisfaction and a sense of fulfillment, a fluidity with life. I feel more aligned with my true nature this way.

Traumatic experiences of loss at an early age, far from blocking me, have developed my empathy skills, knowing that compassion is my fundamental element of analysis. I learned not to judge anything, and above all, not to judge myself. This has greatly benefited my work as a therapist. This natural way of connecting with pain, psychological suffering, and the bodily suffering, with an emotional system extensively introspected over 20 years, led me to direct my interest to the processes of personal transmutation and transformation, of breakdown and reinvention, what is today called deconstruction and reinvention of the self from chaos.

My calling, purpose, and mission in this life has been and is to contribute to the empowerment of people, fostering their self-love, confidence, and ability to joyfully create their own life plans. For several years, my entrepreneurial journey depended on the support of my surroundings: family, friends, and colleagues. Back then, what others thought of me was more important than what I was able to recognize and validate within myself. I found it difficult to stop listening to everyone's voice, forgetting the most important voice – my own.

Until an unexpected turn of events caught me by surprise, and I had no choice. Either I returned to myself or I was put on hold forever. So, I set my creativity and imagination in motion. I had something to sustain me internally and a huge driving force – my daughter.

Meanwhile I was weaving together almost all the versions of my being and integrating them: love, motherhood, my profession, and passions, what my body physically needed to support others, what I am good at, enjoyment, and the painful processes that should have hurt and had been put on hold.

I've never liked being told how to think or what to do. I love being free in my mind and in my choices. I also don't connect superficially with my surroundings, which has earned me more than one criticism and several negative labels.

I take my life very seriously and value intimacy, as well as time with myself as my most precious treasure. This space has shown me that resilient phoenixes are born from great emotional trauma, ready to teach the world their beauty and wisdom.

I consider myself generous of spirit, passionate about self-knowledge and personal growth.

Throughout my life, I have searched for answers and tools that would allow me to live more aligned with my true nature.

Apprehension isn't my thing. Quite the opposite. I've let go of spaces, connections, projects, and material possessions, remaining absolutely faithful to who I am and what I feel. However, I've always received more than what I "lost." The fact is that I'm not afraid of losing. I learned this very early on. And I know that nothing is truly lost. What is not there is for our greatest good.

So, dear reader, my only goal here is to share all these experiences and knowledge with you to help you find your own path to transformationand fulfillment; to motivate you to deeply value simplicity, joy, and genuine pleasure in life; to view the situations you face with greater love; to encour-age you to receive them from a place of non-judgment.

May you trust in the importance of maintaining a positive attitude and in each of our abilities to overcome challenges; connecting with who we truly are; to achieve the dreams we desire; and knowing that we are all truly connected to what our inner truth tells us, even if we don't want to realize it.

I encourage you to feel that connection with the profound, even if it means changing your entire life and leaving people, situations, patterns of behavior, or places behind.

Don't build castles in the air.

Be your true, unedited truth; don't suppress yourself just to please others. Don't be insurmountable or play power games that ultimately lead you nowhere and only hurt you more.

Testimonial

I hope life continues to give you the strength you've always shown to keep moving forward. Beyond your profession, you are, above all, a person who brings joy and happiness to others.

It's also very important to highlight your brilliance at all times, and the generosity of seeking to make others shine before yourself.

I greatly value your professionalism, your integrity, and your strong conviction to see life simply, with joy and sincere pleasure.

Gustavo Schefer
Construction Engineer
Telecommunications

Introduction

What if what you think is an obstacle in your life is actually the gateway to your greatest potential? What if it wasn't about learning something new, but rather recognizing what you already know deep within?

This book was born from that premise and seeks to accompany you on a journey of empowerment and consciousness, where each sentence is a reflection of real transformations.

We live in a world where we've been taught to view our difficulties as obstacles, when in reality they're the key to accessing our true potential. Many people feel trapped in limiting patterns, in beliefs that condition their choices. This book offers a different path: instead of fighting against who we are, it invites you to recognize it, embrace it, and, from there, choose freely.

The reflections and tools contained in these pages are not mere philosophical ideas. They are the result of more than 20 years of clinical care, with more than 40,000 patients treated and a 90% success rate in achieving their goals.

I've seen how interventions in analysis can open doors that seemed sealed. A question can unlock spaces of possibility that were available and simply not recognized, beginning a profound process of change and real expansion.

This book is for anyone who wants to break out of autopilot and access a full, expansive, and conscious life. It's done with kindness and without judgment – internal or external.

No matter your age or stage of life, if you've ever wondered, "What else is possible for me," this book has something for you.

Throughout my professional practice, I have accompanied people like you through their experiences of despair, deception, pain, anger, blockage, frustration, terminal illness, loss, unrequited love, guilt, abuse, and/or violence.

What I share here is not empty theory, but rather tools that have proven effective in unlocking human potential. In a world where stress, anxiety, consumerism, and dissatisfaction are increasingly common, having elements that allow us to deprogram ourselves and make conscious choices is essential.

There are no coincidences. And the people we meet in life, as well as the situations we go through, come to show us something. Something greater than our immediate capacity for understanding, as it brings with it an expansion of consciousness for which, at that moment, we may not yet be ready. I only ask that you be patient. That you trust in life. And finally, with a little perspective, allow yourself to receive the hidden blessings. It is up to you to see each journey as a bridge or an anchor.

I Only Tell the Truth doesn't seek to provide absolute answers, but rather to help you find your own truth, the one that already exists within you and needs to be acknowledged. The truth that gives meaning to your existence, that tells your breathing that you're going in the right direction, that allows you to sleep peacefully and wake up with hope the next day.

Numerous studies in neuroscience, psychology, and epigenetics have shown how our environments, beliefs, and thoughts influence and modify internal biology, changing the way we experience our existence. The tools I share align with these findings, allowing you to rewrite your reality from a new perspective.

Through these brief and powerful stories, this book invites you to question what you take for granted as absolute truth and open yourself to new possibilities. Rather than offering rigid solutions, it offers questions and reflections that facilitate a dynamic and transformative process of self-discovery.

A quick and in-depth read, this book isn't meant to be an in-struction manual, but rather a space for exploration that invites you to recognize your own power and transform yourself based on what works for you.

I invite you to begin this journey. But before you continue reading, I'd like you to let your inspiration flow with the following question:

"IF WE DIDN'T HAVE TO LEARN ANYTHING, BUT SIMPLY RECOGNIZE SOMETHING WITHIN OURSELVES AND KNOW WHAT IS TRUE FOR EACH OF US AND CHOOSE FROM THERE, WHAT WOULD THIS CREATE IN YOUR LIFE OR MINE?"

Prologue

Have you ever felt the overwhelming desire to run away, kick the dashboard, or swerve? This need for change has kept human beings believing and creating for centuries, in search of new paths to a more fulfilling and joyful existence. The motivation for writing this book stems from the experiences of my patients in analysis, my interventions, and the valuable contribution they made to their lives in initiating these profound processes.

Throughout my career, I've had the privilege of guiding many people through their self-discovery and personal transformation. I've witnessed how, through attentive listening and introspective conversation, they've overcome challenges, found clarity, and lived more authentic and happy lives.

Throughout this journey, my own personal experience has been a source of inspiration for them, for me, and for the creation of this book.

Since I was a child, I have delved into my own darkness, overcome my own ghosts, and been reborn in self-discovery. I have faced challenges and learned valuable lessons. These experiences have allowed me to better understand the complexities of the human mind and the importance of living with coherence, presence, authenticity, and peace.

I Only Tell the Truth is born from these unique experiences, mutual growth, and respectful affection. Its purpose is to offer a dynamic and re-laxed perspective that can help others on their own path of personal evolu-tion. I hope that by sharing these stories and considerations, they may inspire you to explore your own truths and live more aligned with your true nature.

Every day, we face situations that plunge us into that heartbreaking desire to change. This book is born from that need, from the constant search for answers and the transformative will that has guided my life up to this point. Moments that change the course of a life forever, and only by taking perspective can we appreciate the hidden blessings they bring to our existence.

Throughout these pages, I will invite you to explore various emotions, tools, and approaches that will allow you to better understand your potential, overcome the challenges that the path poses for our evolution, and understand the way we interact with the world.

Every being is a unique human design, and here I'm going to show you how we are all a constant contribution, whether we know it or not, whether we choose it or it just happens.

The consciousness manifested in each chapter is designed to offer you valuable insights and practical strategies for living more aligned with your being.

There is no life without coherence. The other is survival.

The purpose of this book is to cheer you on your own journey toward truth, self-knowledge, and personal transformation, helping you set clear goals, adopt healthy habits, and find that gentle support to help you recognize, validate, and expand your life in a balanced and purposeful way.

How do you change little by little? How do you choose a different life without that change causing chaos?

Entropy is the concept derived from thermodynamics according to which systems tend to decline toward a state of chaos and disorder. Psychologists use it to describe the amount of uncertainty and disorder that exists in the psyche, despite the rational mind's constant attempt to maintain homeostasis. Physics and psychology are not so far removed from each other. This natural tendency toward disorder can be challenging, but with proper planning, a flexible attitude, and dynamic choices, it is possible to create significant and beneficial changes in your life.

I hope you find in these pages a friendly inspiration to embark on your own path of change and growth. Every small step counts, and in the end, the journey is as important as the destination.

I hope you feel at least intrigued as you turn each page. This small creation carries a positive and expansive vision of life, and seeks to be an invitation to connect with your inner power and the magic of life.

I am aware that my gift may be deep and introspective – even honest and terrifying. Don't expect it to be all laughs. However, I promise you'll leave at least inspired.

My goal is to save you a lot of trouble and help you exorcise the ghosts we all have by helping you with transformative questioning.

I Only Tell the Truth is a book born from the heart of pain and love.

It doesn't offer you "absolute truths," only tools to help you find your own.

It seeks to encourage you to live in the questions that open up possibilities; definitions kill them. It seeks to initiate your own process of introspection and that journey we call access to consciousness in daily life.

Chapter 1: Fear

If you're going to tell your story, let it be one that inspires ...

You fear, which is the reverse of self-love. Fear is not the enemy. Fear is a sign of a lack of freedom and a driving force for growth.

(losses, grief and resignifications)

When we lose someone, sometimes we are old enough to remember, but perhaps not old enough to understand.

Don't be scared, don't be afraid. Fear is not your enemy. Stay calm, it's all in your mind. And if terror takes hold of you even when you're calm, don't wait to be rescued. Your life is your responsibility. Your health is your responsibility, too. Your emotions and thoughts are yours, too.

It doesn't matter who you love, whether you're alone or surrounded by people in your life right now. The only reality is that the one who can pull you out of that place of paralysis, fear, uncertainty, or anxiety is you.

We're not taught this as children; on the contrary, we're taught to depend emotionally, physically, and materially on others. And as adults, this turns us into free beings, afraid to exercise our freedom. Afraid to choose.

We are birds with intentionally broken wings. Not out of malice, but out of ignorance.

Let's be serious: who cares or chooses to care about the depths of their psyche? Most people, most of the time, base their entire life's choices on the seven percent of available knowledge: the mind. When there's much more knowledge within you, usable but untapped, and also better suited to fulfilling your goals and purpose in line with who you are, in the remaining 93 percent. The psyche.

What it's all about, my friend, is being in a good frame of mind, having fun, and letting whatever happens happen. Facing adversity when it's our turn.

The first time I felt fear in my life was when I was 6 years old. I was watching a Michael Jackson zombie movie and thought my 9-year-old brother would turn into one. I later studied the fear of separation in the Faculty of Psychology, in a course called "Individual Psychology of the Subject."

Separation anxiety, or fear, is an intense emotional response that some of us experience when faced with the possibility of being away from significant people in our lives, such as our parents.

I remember that night, for some reason, my parents had gone out alone, leaving us in the care of my older siblings – my younger sister and me. And at that moment, I remember experiencing separation anxiety or terror for the first time.

My family at that time consisted of my father – the breadwinner, a physically and emotionally strong figure; my mother – a woman dedicated to parenting and at home 24/7; my four older siblings; and the two of us, "the girls." It's curious how words impact us from the moment we are born, shaping our choices, personalities, and future development.

The second time I felt like my life was over-paralyzed was when I was 15. I had gone to a friend's 15th birthday party. My father had gone on a trip to train a young pilot who had acquired a helicopter (by the way, my father was a helicopter pilot and flight instructor). Something told me internally that this would be the last time I would see him. The next day, we were informed that there had been an accident. A day later, we were informed my father had died.

I remember what happened to me – a paralysis of that news. It wasn't the thought that he had died, but the thought that he could still be alive, but damaged. My father was a man who took care of everything and everyone – one of those people you could ask to bring you the moon and, without realizing it, he would bring it back. He was a man with a very strong personality. Self-taught, raised by a rural family and without finishing high school, he knew how to make his way in a world as closed as military aviation. Upright. Decisive. And also very strict.

At 15, I thought, as the hours passed and very little information arrived, *What if he becomes paralyzed? What if he can't work? What if he has to be taken care of for life?*

Years later, thanks to psychotherapy, I understood that my terror was about losing that appearance of strength and integrity that he provided to the entire family. "The provider."

And I also understood that in that accident I lost more than a father, more than a paternal semblance. A maternal figure sustained by that powerful husband, disintegrated. "The nurturing mother." She simply stopped supporting us. She became a daughter. And we began to take care of her because, according to my brothers, "she was fragile;" "she could not do it alone;" she did not have the thought process of "I had to do it now that Dad was no longer here."

In addition, in that tragedy, I lost three wonderful companions: two brothers and a mother. My two brothers began to replace my father's roll, and stopped being brothers. And my mother who locked herself away in her grief and isolated herself from everything and everyone.

But "the girls," the youngest daughters and those closest in age, we became a pillar of strength for one another.

When one experiences such significant losses in life, either the calluses become harder and your personality changes, or you use those losses as human capital to contribute to the lives of others.

I did the latter, thanks to my first analyst, Dora Bartolossi, who literally saved my life.

I accepted that each of us did what we felt and could, given our ages, and that processes are individual. I also understood that while grief lasts approximately two years, when the family system transforms and the absence is not registered, that grief can extend for more than 20. This is what we call pathological grief. And each member of the system continues to function as if that figure were still alive.

You can never maintain the same dynamic when someone dies. We absolutely must reinvent and redesign ourselves. And perhaps recording that absence is the most painful thing we can experience.

The third moment of fear and paralysis was when my daughter's father informed me, on the day of our little girl's birth that Lulu, who was born with Down syndrome, and what was even worse, she had congenital heart disease, which led to surgery when she was just 5 months old.

My pregnancy went well, and all the checkups were "normal." The news came the day I gave birth. And I thought, What am I going to do? How is she going to survive in this world? I know nothing about Down syndrome. Who is going to help me? How am I going to raise her alone without a job? I have no more strength. And I cried... I cried and... I cried.

With those questions, I began to grieve for my dream daughter and began to welcome my real daughter. The one who had been with me since 9:15 a.m. on that July 12, 2011. That little lioness who dared to come out into the world, to show us that a person's strength doesn't depend on the oppression we inflict on others, but rather, strength lies in the ability to love others despite the harm they cause us.

It was around 7 p.m. that day when I was able to calm down and finally hold my daughter in my arms. I managed to see her, and she looked at me with her blue eyes, snuggled into my chest, and I felt her warmth. That's when I knew "everything was going to be okay."

The fear and paralysis disappeared, and an inner strength I'd never felt before took hold of both of us and enveloped us. I perceived it clearly. Love is the reverse of fear.

That day I understood that the only thing that counteracts paralysis, terror, uncertainty, or fear is a deep love for life, for living, for oneself, and for those we love.

Until I was 33, I was one person. From then on, I became a different person. Aware, present, and fearless.

Everything began to take on a different meaning, and love filled my soul with strength. Nights and days in the hospital, stays, rehabilitation therapies, open-heart surgery, consultations with various medical specialists, exhaustion, nights sleeping sitting up with my baby in my arms so she wouldn't lack oxygen, stress, anguish – absolutely everything was covered by a blanket of love between us. I had never felt that before. Not even when my father was alive.

That force that drives you forward with courage and determination. That light that rises from the center of your womb and explodes in your chest, encompassing everything you are and do.

That tiny, fragile being who chose me as her mother, through the act of being born, filled my life with such a profound sense of love that any terror, fear of the future, belief that I wouldn't be able to, or unresolved grief from my adolescence were healed.

There I saw him – in those serene and deep blue eyes – my father. And there I knew that the thousands of questions I had anguishly asked him since his physical loss had been answered. Energy is never lost. Energy is transmuted. We never lose those we love. Their energy is transformed into someone or something else.

The loss of a child can be one of the most devastating experiences a person can go through in their life. My daughter is with me. But I know what it means and how much we redefine ourselves internally when going through something like this. I've been with many women through the physical loss of their children.

Grieving a child can be extremely complex and prolonged. Each person experiences it differently, and it's natural to experience profound sadness, disbelief, anger, and a sense of existential emptiness.

In my own grief process, it was crucial to have a support network of friends, therapists, and the rest of my family who could support me, because generally everyone goes through grief.

Sharing your pain with others who have gone through similar experiences can sometimes be incredibly healing.

Losing a parental figure is also a deeply painful experience, although of a very different nature. The loss of parents causes a person to re-evaluate their identity and role within a family. Adult children often take on new responsibilities and roles after such a loss.

Grief is a process that takes time. And it's important to be patient and compassionate with yourself as you go through this difficult journey. Above all, give yourself love. Be kind and listen. Without judgment. We're all doing the best we can.

Today I know that these experiences showed me a path: to choose to accompany my patients, knowing that grief can strengthen emotional resilience, guiding others to face adversity and find new ways to redefine life.

The experiences of loss increased my empathy and understanding for others. Sharing pain can create deeper and more meaningful connections in our daily lives. Everything I went through during those years of grief – only I know – showed me how fragile we can be and, at the same time, how much strength can be born from loving the preciousness of life.

In my life, there's nothing more precious than time, meaningfully shared present moments, and genuine connections. I've learned to accept other people's choices, even if they're far from what I would do. And not to judge them.

I've learned to appreciate adversity as a teacher who teaches me to discover new strengths and perspectives on my own existence and that of others. I've learned to heal within myself what the system hides, resists, or denies.

NOW I KNOW THAT PEACE DOESN'T COME

WHEN EVERYTHING IS FINE, BUT WHEN WE ACCEPT WHAT IS.

Self-Love Exercise

Find a quiet place where you can be alone, without distractions. Take a few minutes to breathe deeply. Relax.

Think about a significant loss you've experienced, whether it was the loss of a loved one, a relationship, or a stage in your life. Write it down in detail: What did you feel? How did it affect you? What did you learn from that experience?

How fear influences your life. Write about a situation in which fear limited or held you back. Then, write about a situation in which love inspired you to act despite your fear. What differences do you find between the two experiences?

Loss and grief have contributed to your personal growth. In what ways have you become stronger, more resilient, or more compassionate? Write them down in detail.

Make a list of things you're grateful for, even in the midst of loss. This will help you find a balance between grief and appreciation for life.

Can you transform fear into a motivating force in your life? What valuable experience do you internalize for your losses? How can you honor the memory of those you have lost while moving on with your life?

THANK YOURSELF. End the exercise by performing an act of love toward yourself or someone else. It can be something simple, like writing a thank-you note, hugging yourself, telling yourself how brave you are, calling a loved one, or taking time for self-care.

This exercise seeks to help you integrate the lessons of grief, loss, and fear as the flip side of love into your life, promoting greater understanding and personal growth.

ASK: If today you found a box with everything you lost in your life up to now, and with all the fears that paralyzed you, what would you do with them?

ANSWER: _____

_____

_____

_____

_____

_____

_____

KEY TRUTH: If you're going to tell your story, let it be to inspire others. Let your words be a reflection of resilience, forgiveness, acceptance, and love. Every experience is an invitation to know more of ourselves.

Chapter 2: Choosing

My love, no one is coming to save you...

Choice is a muscle that requires training on personal empowerment and leadership.

When we work to create light for others, we naturally illuminate our own path. The world needs people who love themselves and what they do.

Opening a space for codependency in psychotherapy involves damaging its basic principle: "trust that the answer is within you."

It only takes me three sessions to be able to detect the pattern that a person repeats, which is why they are not happy in their life.

I always tell them the same thing, you have to be very brave to challenge yourself mentally and physically, to embrace our vulnerability and still keep going. It takes true courage to pursue your passions and dreams, even at the cost of all the systems you were once a part of no longer being part of you.

This is choosing, this is consciousness, and this implies a process of psychotherapeutic autonomy.

Most of the people around us sweep the dirt under the rug. It's not like that's going to make anything better. It's what we call denial. But ignoring the dirt doesn't mean it's not under the rug. And sooner or later, what you deny comes to you and tells you (sometimes not very nicely): either you deal with it or I'll deal with it.

"...for several months I attended therapeutic sessions, which were fundamental in my transition process after a separation of almost ten years of marriage. During this time, we worked both in individual sessions and joint sessions with my ex-wife. This dual approach allowed me to approach and process the separation from different perspectives, facilitating a deeper understanding of my emotions and needs. The individual sessions were especially valuable for me, as they provided me with a safe space to explore my feelings and thoughts. Through these sessions, I was able to identify and release patterns of behavior and emotions that kept me tied to an already exhausted relationship. The guidance and support were crucial in helping me accept the end of this stage of my life and look to the future with hope and clarity. The joint sessions with my ex-wife also played an important role, which allowed us to communicate more effectively and better understand each other's perspectives and emotions. This process not only facilitated a more amicable separation, but also helped us establish a stronger foundation for our future relationship as a former couple and as parents to our children. In short, therapy was a transformative experience that helped me navigate one of the most difficult times of my life. I am deeply grateful for your professionalism, empathy, and ability to create a safe and constructive therapeutic space."

– Remarks from a patient

Gautama Buddha, also known as Siddharta Gautama, prince, ascetic, meditator, hermit, and spiritual master, was the one who said "with your feet on the ground and your soul in your dreams," and has been a kind of compass when listening to a new consultation with a new patient.

What if you just enjoyed living?

Living in reality means not forming expectations of anything or anyone; that is, not deluding ourselves, not creating mental movies, but simply living in the present with whatever happens in our lives based on the choices we make. Not being deluded means not imagining. It's being in the here and now. Taking action and letting everyone give what they have within themselves to offer.

The greatest problem among human beings comes from the expectations and projections we form regarding the reactions to our actions and the people around us. Choosing to create without points of view and without judgment is a mindfulness skill that helps us focus on the present moment, which is not so easy to manage.

And while there are no magic formulas, everything entails responsibility for oneself and one's own desires, as well as respect for the emotions of others. It's not impossible to achieve. It requires training.

Therefore, this book isn't a recipe book, but rather an invitation to rethink your own story in the script of your life. Basically, it aims to improve interpersonal relationships and personal emotional well-being by keeping in mind:

1. **Letting go**: It's allowing people to act according to their nature without trying to control them or change their behavior. By doing so, we reduce the stress and frustration that comes with trying to influence others. Or expecting them to act the way we would. The other person is someone else, I always say. And what they give you is what they have inside. Nothing is personal.

2. **Let yourself be**: that is, focus on what you yourself can modify, that is, your own choices, reactions, and emotions. This involves taking responsibility for your well-being, rather than depending on the actions or attitudes of others. Their ways of living, thinking, or choosing.

By applying these simple tools, you will focus on the idea of accepting that we can't control anything in life, not the actions or thoughts of other people, nor their choices. However, we can control what we choose to do with them.

Living from this perspective fosters peace of mind and strengthens relationships, allowing us to free ourselves from the need to control and focus on our own personal growth.

Daily life presents challenges and opportunities that require courage and determination. Often, we wait for someone else to come and rescue us from our circumstances or adversities. We blame others for our own denials, for our own choices.

The reality is that we are the ones who have the power to transform our lives. To create and recreate them as many times as we want. Good things don't end quickly, and bad things don't last a lifetime.

Your circumstances are nothing more than the product of your choices. People don't do anything to us. Whatever your inner world is, your life will look like. Do yourself a huge favor and stop giving your time, affection, and gifts to someone who isn't willing to receive them.

To be grateful is receiving and giving self love.

Love others. Love yourself. Because there are people who simply seek to exert control by victimizing themselves. They don't know how or want to learn how to deal with managing their emotions and taking responsibility for their own lives. So they go looking for someone to blame for their failures.

A frustrated person will not only fail to appreciate your gift, but will demand more. DON'T DO THAT TO YOURSELF. YOU DON'T NEED IT. YOU ARE PURE ABUNDANT. AND YOU DID TAKE CARE OF HEALING.

Thank yourself and empower yourself. Take on the responsibility of designing your own life plan and making decisions constantly. Even if it means that some people no longer are part of your future, and new ones accompany us.

It's not about having control over everything, or over others, but rather about recognizing that we have the ability to influence our own destiny. Developing a self-efficacy mindset, trusting in our abilities to face and overcome obstacles.

Leadership entails this skill: the ability to guide ourselves toward specific goals and with certain values. And for this, the process of self-knowledge and constant introspection is vital. A self-leader, a person who develops their life plan, knows how to set clear goals, plans concrete actions, and remains committed to their personal growth on a daily basis. It's not a random thing. In all of this, coherence is – in my understanding of expansion – the only way to see success, realized and aligned with life principles and purposes.

So, my dear reader, don't neglect the coffee you're drinking and then complain about finding it cold. Your life is your responsibility. Your bank account is your responsibility. Your relationships, and the quality of them, are your responsibility, too.

Nothing is personal. Everyone chooses what and how. But stop throwing your dirt on the sidewalk and blaming the weather for it.

Although the ability to make conscious choices isn't always innate – it's a muscle that needs to be exercised – we can and should encourage ourselves to choose in every moment, learn to develop it, and live a less constricted life. Every decision, no matter how small, is an opportunity to strengthen this skill and prosper.

Here are some ways to train your choice muscle:

Empowerment and Leadership Exercise

• Spend a few minutes each day reflecting on the decisions you've made. Were they aligned with your values? What could you have done differently?

• Learn to identify what's truly important to you. This helps you make decisions that are more consistent with who you are and therefore more satisfying.

• Don't be afraid to set your boundaries. Saying "no" when something doesn't resonate with you is about being true to yourself and developing internal/external coherence. Being assertive in your decisions strengthens your ability to fully choose from your voice.

• Not every choice is going to be perfect, and that's okay. Learning from mistakes is part of the growth process.

Being the leader of your own life is like becoming a high-performance athlete in this constant decision-making process. No one is going to save you, but you don't need to be saved. We have within us the strength and wisdom necessary to lead our own life project.

Be proud of who you are becoming and be grateful for yourself. The difference you are isn't right or wrong; it's simply who you are. Breaking out of the loop of searching for what's right or wrong about you and asking what will create this is the beginning of strengthening yourself.

EXERCISE: By exercising the muscle of choice, we become the architects of our future. In turn, each choice is an opportunity to get closer to creating the life you desire and deserve.

Don't stop your life for anyone; only do it if your soul requires it. You are like "David" trapped in marble. Your ultimate goal in life is to remove all those fears, doubts, insecurities, emotions, negative thoughts, and limiting false beliefs that hold you back; until all that remains is the best version of you.

Life belongs to those who want to live it. I'm as sure there's something more, as I am that there's a heaven up there, something even non-believers can believe in.

Life belongs to those who know love is beautiful, love is healthy. There's no other form of love. And without true love, we just exist. So, until you find love within yourself, you'll just be someone without a soul.

Trust me when I tell you that as you walk, let your heart guide your steps and you will return, you will recover, you will find that love (in yourself) where you left it.

Don't forget that "living" is the result of the choices you make.

They should aim for an optimal, holistic, and balanced state of being. And this includes the multiple facets of your existence. Without this constant and conscious balance, life limits its full potential.

Learn to prioritize what's truly important, not what's urgent. That can wait. You came to be happy; stop being distracted by productivity. And being happy is, in principle, accepting and forgiving everything and everyone as they are. It involves relinquishing control and accepting the natural course of life.

In this entire process of choosing whenever necessary, being present is crucial. Turn off autopilot.

THANK YOURSELF: End the exercise by committing to making a different choice today. It doesn't have to be something that scares or challenges you too much. Remember that choosing is an exercise. It requires training. Going from less to more shows your mind that it's possible without blocking it. And do this every day, maintaining it for a month.

This exercise aims to help you learn to train your mind and that muscle called choice. Nothing is static, nor is it permanent. The only constant is change.

ASK: What's this all about? Are we meant to take more than we should? That we give or are meant to be kind? When was the last time you said, "I love you," to yourself in the mirror? Or when you looked into someone's eyes and felt a deep desire to tell them how much you love them?

ANSWER:_____

_____

_____

_____

_____

KEY TRUTH: Choosing is a muscle that requires training. Each decision strengthens our ability to live authentically and with purpose.

Reflect on your values and priorities. What really matters to you in life? What are your non-negotiables?

Identify your strengths and embrace your vulnerability. A deep understanding of all areas of our self helps us make decisions.

Train yourself to make small choices every day. Consciously choosing what to eat, what to wear, how to spend your free time, how you're going to have fun today, prepares us for bigger choices. Never start with something transcendental. And if it doesn't work out, come back to choose again. The biggest limitation is perpetuating choices that don't contribute to us dynamically and meaningfully.

Chapter 3: Healthy Selfishness

Hey, you... Shine! Shine like Oscar De La Renta's strapless dress at Paris Fashion Week because there can always be another love, another job, another place, but never another life.

Healthy selfishness: It's not self-centeredness – How to heal your relationship with yourself.

THREE STORIES, THREE TALES, THREE STRENGTHS

Each patient of mine has come to me at rather complicated times. As their therapist, I always offer a few gentle words as we start their journey together. I know this is a difficult circumstance, so I show them warmth and compassion. My hope is always to motivate my patients and empower them to step out of their comfort corner and begin a journey of healthy selfishness.

What follows are three snippets of patients' stories that tell the tales of getting through the toughest of times and rising to be stronger than ever.

"It was very difficult for me to get out of that dark and negative cloud I had in my head, but with commitment and positivity, I was able to achieve it. You were a beacon of pure light that illuminated the completely dark path I found myself on. Positive, healing. With you, I learned and continue to learn to love myself first, in order to love others. It was an internal growth, several discoveries, and knowing that you can always overcome any situation and change. You helped me take the step of seeing what I didn't see in myself. I opened a huge door that opens wider every day. Constructive. From imbalance to virtuous transformation."

~ ~ ~ ~ ~

"In a few words, it's hard to describe what you mean to me: you're my subconscious that I don't want to listen to, my guide and my support. With you, I made the most important and correct decision. I quit my job as a retail clerk and open my beauty salon, which is still going strong 10 years later. It boosts my self-esteem. I leave feeling like everything will be okay, and I feel calm and liberated. You are so valuable. I feel heard and understood. You help me become a better person."

~ ~ ~ ~ ~

"I would use a very short phrase but it makes a lot of sense to me, the therapy was at the right time. One day you told me: 'You have to change,' while I learned to whisper: 'You are perfect just the way you are. You are enough.'"

~ ~ ~ ~ ~

In these years of interacting with patients, I have heard thousands of stories, and my own analysis for over 20 years. Do you know what I've accepted? That you can spend your life seeking external approval and it will never come. You can spend your life trying to please, satisfy, and assist others, and you will never receive recognition.

I learned that you have no obligation to do anything for anyone. However, you have the human right to do whatever is within your power to be happy.

We didn't come here to suffer. We came here to enjoy this experience that is life. Stay close to those people who make you feel that being yourself is okay.

Don't forget self-love. What you give, you give to yourself. Learn to choose what you give to yourself. Because mental health isn't something you have, it's something contributes to your well-being – your health. And psychotherapy alone isn't enough.

Your life is the result of various choices, from the most insignificant to the most absolutely incredible. And all of them should aim for an optimal, holistic, and balanced state of your BEING, and this includes the multiple facets of your existence. Without that constant and conscious balance in your living, your creative potential, your joy, and the peace that was granted to us at the moment of conception are limited.

Love, there's no time for anything that doesn't have a heart. Stop being distracted by the daily conflict you stuff into your head. You came into this world to be incredibly happy. Believe in yourself. You are enough. Take away the power of everything that disturbs you. If it doesn't exist in your mind, it won't exist in your life either.

Change your point of view and everything will change. Realize that what bothers you is in your own head. It's all lies. Your potential is unlimited. Learn to manage your personal space and make setting boundaries a priority. The simple fact that you are not paying attention to anyone is a great contribution to the world – especially to your self-care.

Because love, before it can be mutual, must be your own. Learn to discern it.

EGOCENTRISM

That attitude or personality trait in which a person is excessively focused on themselves and their own interests, often at the expense of others.

SELF-LOVE

It's not self-centeredness. It's learning to value yourself and prioritize your well-being. It requires that healthy measure of selfishness that allows you to heal your relationship with yourself. It's essential for learning how to manage personal space and set boundaries. Showing your brilliance doesn't mean overshadowing anyone. Showing your authenticity and live fully doesn't mean being indifferent to the person next to you. Allowing yourself to be the star of your own story and embracing your inner light without fear in no way requires shutting anyone down with judgment or criticism. That's insecurity. Lack of confidence in yourself. Lack of self-esteem and self-love.

Be aware that a person's brilliance causes more envy than any material thing, because it's intangible and is closely related to someone's personality and virtues. It can't be bought. Learn to make those around you shine. And if they can't, don't insist. But don't be the repository of all their projections. People have free will and not everyone is willing to love themselves, or knows how to love. It's not your fault. You don't have to endure anything.

FROM EMPOWERMENT TO PERSONAL LEADERSHIP

To empower oneself is to lead the interrelated processes that allow us to live fully, confidently, and assertively. By assuming the design and control of our lives, guiding us with purpose. Achieve a state of balance and comprehensive well-being.

I'm going to tell you everything that empowerment is not:
- It does not involve running over anyone
- It's not about being more than anyone else
- It's not about not nullifying your vulnerability
- It is not denying your finitude
- It is not ignoring the other
- It is not judging the other.

Empowerment is a profound process in which we embrace our shadows, our fissures, and from there, from that vulnerability, we strengthen, integrate, and assume leadership of our own existence. We make conscious and responsible decisions for our well-being and growth, as well as for the well-being of those around us. Even if this means changing structures, resigning roles, or changing actions for permission, or letting go of bonds that hurt us.

It encompasses some key aspects:

• **Self-knowledge**: Knowing our values, interests, and needs is essential for making decisions that make us feel fulfilled and satisfied. Self-knowledge allows us to understand who we are and what we want from life.

• **Self-confidence**: Empowerment involves developing a strong belief in our abilities and skills. Recognizing our achievements and learning from our failures helps us build healthy self-esteem.

• **Personal Responsibility**: Taking responsibility for our actions and decisions is a crucial component of empowerment. We realize that we have the power to influence our destiny and are not dependent on others for our happiness and success.

• **Setting Limits**: Knowing how to say "no" when something doesn't resonate with our values is essential to protecting our emotional and mental well-being. Clear boundaries allow us to prioritize our needs without feeling guilty.

• **Skill Development**: Empowerment also involves acquiring new skills and knowledge. This can include education, professional development, and continuous improvement in areas of interest and passion.

Leading your life involves the ability to guide and direct your own existence with purpose and determination. You will need:

• **A clear vision and goals**: A self-leader has a clear vision of what they want to achieve and sets concrete goals to achieve it. Planning and organization are important tools to keep us on track toward our goals.

• **To plan, perseverance and commitment**: Personal leadership requires discipline to keep moving forward, even when we face challenges. Staying committed to our goals and working consistently helps us move forward.

• **To be open to change and flexible**: Life is full of unexpected changes and challenges. A good personal leader knows how to adapt and be flexible, adjusting their plans as needed to keep moving forward.

• **To make Conscious Decisions**: Making decisions based on our personal values and goals is fundamental to effective leadership. Evaluating options and considering consequences allows us to make informed and consistent decisions.

• **Above all, kindness toward yourself**: Being a leader of our own lives also involves being compassionate with ourselves. Accepting that we're not perfect and that making mistakes is part of the process helps us maintain a positive and resilient attitude.

As the creator of your own life, ask yourself:

Do I focus my energy, time, money and resources to take me to the next level?

Everything in this life teaches. You'll see if you learn. Look for something good, not just in appearance, but something solid, stable, and even more beautiful in its most secret part. It's not far away, you'll find it. You just have to know where to reach.

EXERCISE IN HEALTHY SELFISHNESS AND SELF-LOVE

This exercise will help you clarify your goals, overcome obstacles, and commit to a significant change in your life. I hope it helps you on your transformation journey! If you need more information, support, join my community. I'm here to help.

Find a quiet place where you can be alone and free from distractions. This exercise requires a serene environment in which to reflect deeply.

Mental Preparation: sit down comfortably, close eyes and breathe deeply several times. Repeat this until you feel yourself relaxing; allow your mind to focus solely on the present.

Reflection on the Current State: Take a notebook and write down the answers to the following questions:

• What area of my life do I feel most stuck or needs change?

• What limiting thoughts or beliefs are preventing my growth in this area?

• What negative emotions are associated with this situation?

Visualizing Your Desired Future: Imagine what your life would be like if you could modify those obstacles. Visualize in detail how you would feel, how you would act, and how your environment would change. Write your reflections in your notebook:

• How do I see myself in my desired future?

• What positive emotions bring about this state?

• What skills have I developed?

Identifying Concrete Steps: Based on your visualization, write three specific actions you can take to get closer to your desired future. Make sure they're concrete and achievable:

• What can I do today to begin this change?

• What habits do I need to develop or change?

• What support or resources do I need to achieve this?

Commitment to Change: Write a letter to yourself,committing yourself to follow these steps. Read the letter aloud and keep it somewhere you can see it regularly to remind yourself of your commitment to your transformation.

Review and Adjust: Schedule time each week to review your progress and adjust your actions as needed. Reflect on what you've learned and celebrate your achievements, no matter how small.

THANK YOURSELF. Finish the exercise as you began the chapter. In front of a full-length mirror, you're going to repeat this phrase until you can meet your own gaze. Don't be embarrassed to say it.

"Shine stupid!" Shine like a strapless sequined scallop column gown by Oscar De La Renta at Paris Fashion Week because there can always be another love, another job, other places, but never another life."

This exercise aims to help you learn to recognize the brilliance within you – your uniqueness – the valuable being that you are.

You are a unique gift to the world. Don't dim your light for anything or anyone. And to anyone who isn't comfortable with your brilliance, give them a pair of Gucci sunglasses!

ASK: If I were truly being myself, what would I choose today? What choice am I going to make today that will create something greater in my life? How can I have more fun with the choices I'm making now? And if choosing wasn't forever, but only for the next ten seconds, what choices would I be allowing myself to make?

ANSWER:_____

_____

_____

_____

_____

_____

KEY TRUTH: "Healthy selfishness isn't self-centeredness. It's the art of taking care of ourselves and prioritizing our own well-being, so we can offer something great of ourselves to others."

Taking care of your health is necessary: It is not possible to link our health without being physically, emotionally and mentally linked. Move your body regularly, don't eat, learn to nourish yourself; it's very different. Get enough rest. Prioritizing your well-being allows you to be optimally prepared to tackle life's challenges and choosing efficiently. These are all selfishly healthy acts.

Setting boundaries helps you manage your personal space: Taking care of your non-negotiables, that is, establishing your "no" when you really don't or can't do something. This is a form of proper personal space management. This way, you protect your time and energy so you can focus on what really matters.

Taking time for yourself: Devoting time to activities you enjoy, such as reading, practicing a hobby, or simply relaxing, is essential for maintaining your self-esteem, energy, and emotional balance.

Seek help when you need it: Whether it's talking to a trusted friend, seeking professional support, or joining a group, recognizing that you need help for emotional support and seeking it is an act of self-care and healthy selfishness.

It's a priority to give relevance to your emotions. Allow yourself to feel and express them, and learn to communicate them for your overall well-being.

Investing in personal development: Attending training, workshops, or reading books that help you grow personally and professionally allows you to move forward and feel fulfilled.

Practice self-reflection: Take some time every day to reflect on your goals, values, and priorities. This will help you align your thoughts with your choices and the actions to achieve them. It's the principle of consistency that will expand your life.

Chapter 4: Guilt

THE BLAME: a large distracting implant

It took you a long time to heal. Be selective about who has access to you. Not everyone deserves your new version. Break free from the past without burdening yourself with the judgments of others.

Have you ever heard of them? The **distractor** implants?

They act like dogs chasing their tails. What do I mean by this? Well, when dogs chase their tails, they entertain themselves, but they never get anywhere and very few are actually successful in catching their tails.

So, the purpose of distracting implants is to prevent us from being ourselves – to be present in our lives and with our choices. And they do their job very well! Because the deeper we sink into the mire of a distracting implant, the harder it is to see that we have any options other than what our mind tells us.

Do you already have an idea of what they are? Anger, rage, fury, guilt, shame, remorse, doubt, fear, dread, forgiveness, love, healing – these are just some of the 24 distracting implants that help us avoid taking responsibility for our daily choices and victimize ourselves to control others.

Revealing? Hard, maybe. That's how true it is.

The bright side of this truth is that when you can identify them and identify yourself in this role without judging yourself, your mind relaxes, changes and deprograms, your body, too, and you begin to make choices for something greater for you. You locate in a more generous place to create your life.

Reflect for a second on the following:

How many people you know tell you they are victims and use that to victimize themselves and control you?

Most people who say they're victims use this to exert some control over your life and the lives of those around them, and thus achieve their own personal goals – becoming the victimizer who controls you. Unconsciously, what they're telling you is: *"I've been abused so you need to take care of me."*

How many of you have tried to care for someone who was a victim? It never works, right? Or does it?

The only underlying motive of the victim/victimizer, blame/guilty pair is to seek attention without emotional responsibility. Up to a certain age, there is someone else who requires our care; after that period, caregiving becomes an individual responsibility. Throughout childhood and adolescence, our parents or caregivers are the ones who protect us (or should) and provide us with the tools to fully develop into adulthood. This function, then, becomes a purely personal exercise.

From Guilt to Forgiveness

According to Sigmund Freud, guilt is an emotion deeply rooted in our psyche and is related to the conflict established between the desires of the unconscious, the ego that enunciates them, and the superego created in the image and likeness of social and family mandates.

The unconscious is the most primitive part of our mind, driven by instinctive desires and needs. The ego acts as a mediator between these and the restrictions of reality. The superego represents our moral conscience, shaped by society and our experiences.

Freud believed that guilt arises when the ego fails to mediate correctly and align the desires of the unconscious with the moral norms that society imposes as mandates. Then one or the other becomes tyrant.

This lack of balance can lead to feelings of self-criticism and self-accusation, which are incredibly destructive. So much so that it can cause us to develop disorders such as compulsive disorders, such as depressive symptoms, and in rare and extreme cases, perversions of desires. Parenthetically, for Freud, depression was an extreme form of guilt that entails an exaggerated form of self-criticism and self-harm. A form of guilt directed toward oneself.

It is in his iconic work "Mourning and Melancholy" (1917), where he describes and explores how guilt is rooted in both individual life and culture, considering it a "dark face" that creeps deep into the mental life of the individual and the history of culture.

Guilt arises because the ego fails to satisfy the desires of the unconscious without transgressing the norms imposed by the superego. This generates a feeling of intense internal discomfort and exaggerated self-criticism. Culture has a significant influence on our perception and handling of guilt. These concepts vary considerably across different cultures and societies, and our personal experience with them is profoundly influenced by the family and cultural environment in which we grew up and developed.

FROM GUILT TO HONOR

Modern psychology considers forgiveness a powerful tool for emotional and mental well-being. It helps us let go of resentment and revenge and adopt an attitude of understanding, compassion, and empathy toward others and, most importantly, toward ourselves.

From a Freudian and classical psychology perspective, forgiveness is a way beyond guilt. It implies a reconciliation between the ego, the unconscious, and the superego – the three psychic instances that make up the human psyche. In other words, it is not only a tool that allows us to free ourselves from guilt, but also to find emotional and moral balance within ourselves. This process necessarily entails the revision of mandates, ideals, cultural values, questioning, and the creation of new registers more adapted to our true selves.

Although Freud did not specifically dedicate his work to the topic of forgiveness, this perspective can be inferred from his general theories about the human psyche.

In this way, as I explained above, forgiveness would be directly related to the three levels of the psyche: the unconscious, the ego, and the superego. The unconscious houses repressed desires and conflicts, while the ego tries to mediate between these desires and the demands of reality, and the superego acts as the voice of internalized morality and ethics. Forgiveness, in this context, could be seen as a process of freeing the mind from the guilt and tension that arise from the inherent conflict between these three components. By forgiving, one could reconcile these internal conflicts and find a kind of psychological balance.

Furthermore, Freud understood that many human emotions and behaviors, including the capacity to forgive, are deeply informed by childhood experiences and early relationships with authority figures, such as our parents or caregivers.

More generally, although Freud didn't write extensively about this concept, it *might work* in terms of releasing guilt and resolving internal conflicts. Therefore, psychology considers it a tool for mental and emotional health. It helps individuals release remorse, resentment, and bitterness, leading them to adopt a more kind attitude toward themselves and others.

I will develop more on this later, but it's worth emphasizing that forgiveness is a complicated topic. If it works as part of a healing process in a therapeutic setting for the victim (of violence, abuse, or alienation), it's acceptable. However, we can never impose this tool on a patient who is part of a structure that attempts to maintain harmony and the status quo in a completely iatrogenic or perverse family as part of the cure in a therapeutic process.

From Honor to Self-love

Many religions have specific teachings about guilt and forgiveness. For example, in Christianity, guilt is linked to the concept of sin, and forgiveness is obtained through confession and repentance. In Buddhism, guilt can be related to the concept of karma, and the focus is on spiritual purification and continuous improvement.

In cultures like Africa, forgiveness is an integral part of the reconciliation process. Restorative justice processes emphasize forgiveness and community reconciliation to preserve social balance and peace. In contrast, in more legalistic cultures like China, forgiveness may be viewed as a sign of weakness or an abdication of justice. Punishment may be more valued than the act of forgiveness, in order to preserve social homeostasis and hierarchies.

In many cultures, forgiveness remains deeply linked to honor and shame. In these societies, forgiving someone is seen as restoring lost honor, while unforgiveness is seen as a way to maintain prestige.

Throughout history, the concept of honor has been fundamental in the construction of individual and collective identity. Traditionally, honor was linked to the fulfillment of social duties, loyalty to the community, and adherence to established norms. It was an external virtue, bestowed by society in recognition of behavior considered worthy and exemplary.

Self-love, on the other hand, is born from recognizing and appreciating one's own intrinsic dignity, independent of social approval. It involves cultivating a healthy relationship with oneself, based on respect, compassion, and authenticity. This approach not only promotes individual well-being but also lays the foundation for more genuine and equitable relationships with others.

The transition from honor to self-respect does not mean rejecting traditional values, but reinterpret them from a more introspective and conscious perspective. By integrating self-respect with respect for others, a personal ethic is built that harmonizes individual responsibility with collective empathy.

In this process of transformation, the individual becomes the primary agent of his or her own development, guided by an internal compass that values both personal integrity and the common good. Thus, self-love emerges as a liberating force that empowers human beings to live fully and consistently with their deepest values.

THE BONDS WE ATTRACT ARE A MIRROR OF OUR OWN CHILDHOOD

Often our bonds reflect and mirror the experiences and dynamics of our own childhood. From a young age, our experiences with our parents and caregivers shape our beliefs and expectations about relationships, as well as creating lifelong imprints that remain in our psyche, veiled by other experiences. And it's on this basis that in adulthood we form bonds, believing that our choices are random. Or, even funnier, conscious.

If you grew up in a loving and secure environment, you likely seek out and attract similar bonds. On the other hand, if your childhood was marked by conflict or lack of affection, you may find that you attract bonds that replicate these same patterns. Recognizing them is the first step toward transformation. By understanding how your childhood has influenced your current choices, you can start making more conscious and, above all, healthier decisions.

We often confuse loyalty with absolute permanence by someone or something's side, enduring all sorts of horrible things. But this isn't loyalty because your common sense doesn't tell you the same thing. And there's a primitive instinct in all living beings that tells us yes and no. Loyalty doesn't depend on circumstances, but on human values and principles.

Waking up next to someone we say we're staying with out of loyalty, when in reality it's because of a lack of boundaries, is giving away our ability to leave or let them go. Our choices create our situations. We can create love, respect, honesty, empathy, peace, kindness, abundance, or chaos, arrogance, lies, destruction, meanness, shouting, pain, and illness.

Just look at the world to realize this. You'll see how much energy we have. Do you want to live together daily? But remember the following: no one gives what doesn't live inside.

Don't be fooled by your own words or those of others. And when you feel doubt, I suggest you do like the deaf, turn off your ears and just observe the actions. There you will find all the answers. What's in your mind is what makes your body sick, and vice versa.

You are enough. Avoid all comparisons like a plague. Do not compare yourself to anyone. And follow what feels good to you in this moment and every moment. That will create a wonderful life for you. No romantic relationship, no family bond, no friendship, or professional relationship is worth as much as your health and peace of mind.

THE MOST GENEROUS SELFISH ACT YOU CAN DO FOR OTHERS IS TO LOVE YOURSELF SO MUCH THAT EVERYONE AROUND YOU HAS NO DOUBT ABOUT WHAT YOUR NON-NEGOTIABLES ARE.

And only adventure into a relationship if your life is better and greater being in it than without it. But don't lose sight of the fact that even before that, the best and greatest relationship you have. What you should strive to build is with yourself. And this is achieved by preserving within yourself what we call the elements of intimacy: honor, trust, gratitude, vulnerability, and permission. And if you add to this these three components that I'm going to tell you about below to create – and notice that I wrote "create" and "not have" – a bond, which is also significantly different, since the relationship speaks of the distance between point A and point B – the bond will then be a great conscious creation. When we relate, we separate ourselves from the other. When we connect, we generate a dialectic hold. Keep this in mind when making connections with your surroundings and you will notice a big difference.

I was telling you there are three elements that would be interesting for you to explore before immersing yourself in the world of connecting significantly with another/others.

1. the person/s is/are good at sex

2. earns money

3. does not hinder your desires, and vice versa.

If you've already shared the five elements of intimacy with us, then you're in for a truly joyful experience together. Don't rush. I know it's a lot of new information in just a few paragraphs. Let's explore everything together.

IF YOU WANT TO SEE BUTTERFLIES,

TAKE CARE OF THE PLANTS IN YOUR GARDEN.

Let's call this patient "Yara."

She had always lived in fear of expressing herself. Fearing what people would say. Internally holding onto family mandates that clearly didn't make her happy, but which she couldn't help but try to please. And it was never enough, of course. Like everything that happens in the field of relationships. Every time she wanted to speak in a meeting with her team or bosses, she would be quiet; she avoided her husband directly; with friends her words were drowned in gossip and then she directed her attention to anything else in order to get out of the presence of her own life; she would say everything "always" was fine. I often watched her say "yes" when she wanted to scream "no," and she felt trapped in routines that clearly didn't make her happy or expand her life.

Very gradually, we began to circle around what I call "a greater desire." Small, seemingly insignificant steps that finally led her to connect with her true desire and to anguish over something she herself had erased from her consciousness. Since she was a child, she wanted to help people, and due to family legacy and limiting beliefs, she had resigned and studied another career, also humanitarian but distant, like mental health.

So she returned to college for her second degree, a career she dreamed of pursuing and had abandoned. Another of her great changes, in what I call insinuations of desire, was to return, almost daily, to another of her passions: water and the intimacy that stroke after stroke generated with it. Little by little, she began to find herself. Seeing herself, recording and integrating those fragments of being that life, obligations, impositions, and culture imprint on everyone. And her inner voice began to strengthen and communicate that her contribution was and is valuable.

She was encouraged to share it herself first and then share it with those around her. "Yara" began to feel more present in her life, excited, with that sparkle in her eyes that we only see when someone is being who they truly are. And she laughed again – out loud, in fact.

She began to choose what to do and what to never do again. During the sessions, I witnessed how that garden full of weeds transformed and butterflies of all colors arrived. And one day, she shared her story for the first time with her partner and felt immensely liberated at being heard.

Over time, "Yara" became a source of inspiration for others in her community. She began leading groups and receiving important feedback. Today, she is inspiring the lives of others and working on the importance of living authentically, coherently, and above all, with great kindness toward one's own internal processes, in the office space as a therapist.

The transformation wasn't immediate or easy, but each small step led her to a grander place, of greater personal power within herself. Not everything is resolved. We continue to address presence in her life and decision-making. Some ghosts continue to haunt her, but she knows it's her choice to take that power away and to guide her life to the next level of consciousness.

TRUE FREEDOM COMES WHEN WE STOP EXISTING TO PLEASE OR MEET THE EXPECTATIONS OF OTHERS AND BEGIN LIVING TO FULFILL OUR OWN DESIRES. THAT'S TRANSFORMATION AND REBIRTH. I HOPE YOU MEET PEOPLE WHO SPEAK YOUR LANGUAGE SO YOU DON'T HAVE TO TRANSLATE YOUR SOUL YOUR WHOLE LIFE. AND IF YOU'RE GOING TO DREAM... EXAGGERATE, BECAUSE DREAMS DO COME TRUE.

Transformation Exercise

1. Pattern Identification

• Take a notebook and write down your first relationship experiences. What were your relationships like with your parents or caregivers? What dynamics were repeated?

• Reflect on your current relationships. Do you see similar patterns? For example, you tend to attract people with characteristics similar to those of your parents?

2. Explore your Beliefs

• Write a list of beliefs you have about love and relationships. For example, "Love is difficult to maintain" or "I am not worthy of unconditional love."

• Analyze where these beliefs come from. Are they the result of your childhood experiences?

3. Reframe Limiting Beliefs

• Identify at least one limiting belief and reformulated it into a positive belief. For example, change "Love always leads to pain" to "Love can be a source of joy and growth."

4. Conscious Actions

• Commit to taking a concrete action that reinforces your new belief. For example, if your new belief is "Love can be a source of joy," look for activities or situations that allow you to experience and share joy with others.

5. Reflection and Acceptance

• Reflect on the importance of self-acceptance and self-love. Remember that to attract healthy relationships, you must first cultivate a healthy relationship with yourself.

• Practice self-compassion and allow yourself to feel all your emotions without judgment.

THANK YOURSELF: Finish the exercise as you began the chapter. In front of a full-length mirror, you're going to repeat this phrase until you can meet your own gaze. Don't be embarrassed to say it.

"Shine stupid!" Shine like a strapless sequined scallop column gown by Oscar De La Renta at Paris Fashion Week. Because there can always be another love, another job, other places, but never another life."

This exercise aims to help you learn to recognize the brilliance within you. Your uniqueness. The valuable being you are.

You are a unique gift to the world. Don't dim your light for anything or anyone. And to anyone who isn't comfortable with your brilliance, give them a pair of Gucci sunglasses.

ASK: If I were truly being myself, what would I choose today? What choice am I going to make today that will create something greater in my life? How can I have more fun with the choices I'm making now? And if choosing wasn't forever but only for the next ten seconds, what choices would I be allowing myself to make?

ANSWER:_____

_____

_____

_____

_____

KEY TRUTH: Guilt and forgiveness are great distracting implants. Distractor implants are concepts used in Access Consciousness to describe those thoughts, emotions, and reactions that distract us from being fully aware and present in our lives. These implants can include feelings such as fear, doubt, guilt, regret, and anger.

These implants can rise from various experiences and conditioning throughout our lives, and are designed to keep us trapped in patterns of behavior that prevent us from reaching our true potential and living as who we truly are.

Distractor implants can rise in several ways:

• Social and Cultural Conditioning: From a young age, we are influenced by the norms and expectations of the society and culture we live in. These influences can create distracting implants such as fear, guilt, and self-doubt.

• Traumatic experiences: Traumatic or stressful events can leave a deep mark on our psyche, creating distracting implants that keep us in a constant state of alert or cause us to relive the trauma.

• Limiting Beliefs: The beliefs we adopt about ourselves and the world can become distracting implants. For example, believing that we are not good enough can lead to feelings of insecurity and self-criticism.

• Potential Blocking: Distracting implants can have several negative effects on our lives. They keep us trapped in patterns of behavior and thinking that limit our ability to grow and achieve our goals.

• Stress and Anxiety: Distracting thoughts like fear and guilt can generate high levels of stress and anxiety, affecting our mental and physical health.

• Damaged Relationships: They can interfere with our interpersonal relationships, creating conflicts and misunderstandings.

• Lack of Presence: They distract us from being fully present in the moment, which can affect our ability to enjoy life and make conscious decisions.

To deal with them we can use tools like those provided in previous chapters. Or techniques like "the bars of access to consciousness" that help us recognize and release the energy contained in these distractions, allowing us to be more present and aware in our lives.

Be selective about who accompanies you in this new version of yourself; it took you time to redesign it. Free yourself from other people's judgments. Embrace your self-love. Remember that the quality of your ties reflects the quality of the relationship that you have with yourself."

Chapter 5: Pain

IF I HELP JUST ONE PERSON, I WILL NOT HAVE LIVED IN VAIN.

The pain, a great mentor – Learning from adversity without getting stuck in it.

All the painful experiences I went through in my life made me understand that walking in itself is a constant opportunity to be myself and show the world the gift that I am.

Are you ready to let go of what's been holding you back and begin this new chapter in your life?

Humans go through cycles that psychology understands as evolutionary, as they show us that we are ready to leave behind something that has prevented us from moving forward.

If you came across this book, the answer is yes.

Can you realize that you are ready to live a new cycle in your life?

Your creativity and focused effort will take you to the next level. All those experiences and lessons, the energies that were stagnant, will begin to flow.

Closing Cycles and Starting New Challenges

There are cycle endings that occur every 10 years and show the possibility of banishing habits, wounds, or outdated thoughts that lead nowhere. It may be an opportune moment to face new challenges.

Universal laws teach that what we experience daily in our lives is not a reflection of what we do, but of who we are. However, if you notice that something has begun to be radically different in your daily life, perhaps what is being revealed is the synchronicity of your inner self with your outer self.

Then surely you will find in that moment of searching for what it means or what message you're receiving from all these "coincidences." The transformation of being precedes the transformation of having. Abundance isn't something you conquer; it's something you allow yourself.

It's never about doing more. It's just about becoming more aware that stretching your consciousness is how you access the same capabilities and abilities as the rest of nature.

Flow with the Universe

Anxiety and excessive effort are merely symptoms of a limited understanding of universal laws. They are manifestations of the ego, which believes it has everything under control and attempts to orchestrate what is already divinely ordered. When you understand that you are part of the infinitely generous universe, and that it is abundant by nature, you will stop struggling and begin to flow.

Your True Power

Your power lies not in doing, but in being. It lies not in action, but in presence. It lies not in control but in allowing. By being aware of the divine flow of life, you are being summoned to a quantum leap of consciousness that will shatter all previous limitations of you as a manifestor.

The Key to Manifestation

The question is not whether you will be able to manifest your desires, but how much longer you will resist what is already yours by universal right. Men and women see therapy differently. Even though stereotypes of feminism and machoism have blended through the years, many men still don't dare consider therapy. But I ty to show them the benefits of therapy and most come away with a different perspective.

Here are testimonies from some of my male patients:

"Going to therapy with you was a turning point, a lifesaver for me, my partner, and my family. It made me return to the roots of which I was in the beginning, understanding that life is simple and that one's choices are fundamental to living happily. It helped me remove toxic people from my life, enjoy what I love, and stop lying to myself to mask situations with the outside world..."

"You contain yourself emotionally. You taught me to understand and listen to myself much more, as well as to my body..."

"From the day I decided to start with you, endless possibilities presented themselves in my mind. I felt a sense of freedom, love, and support in this new stage of my life. Thank you so much..."

"Well, without being able to express it in many words, meeting you was a 180-degree turn in my life. I hit rock bottom, and that's why I decided to seek outside help, in addition to family support. I must say that after that, I was able to gain a much broader perspective than I had before, managing the problems or situations that arose in my later life in a different way, with many of the tools you gave me, making it much more enjoyable for my emotional stability. I would like to thank you very much for your dedication to helping each of your patients – in this case, me – improve my quality of life..."

"Two words: No return. It only depends on me and my choices..."

"Sincerity and learning come to mind and trigger other things. Sincerity; because with you I felt confident not to hold anything back, to be able to talk and tell EVERYTHING. And that's liberating. It gives inner strength. You generate that. And it's very good. And learning: because it helped me and helps me live better. Therapy is for that. Because I was able to tell you who I am, because you intervened, you taught me with clear words and examples, and that helped me in my daily life. I feel and live better thanks to the therapy I've had with you..."

"It was an incredible, complete transformation. An experience I would repeat if I could go back in time. Everything I am today, I owe to our 10 years of therapy together. I'd close by saying it was a wonderful experience…"

"My transformation experience with you was totally positive. I found myself again. I got up and believed in myself. I regained the positive energy that characterized me, and now I'm super empowered. I feel like there's no limit to what I set my mind to, and that's thanks to psychotherapy with you. I can achieve everything I desire in my life. I'm always honest, and the truth is, if I didn't go further, it's because you helped me so much. Especially to value myself, which is what took me a long time to understand..."

"My time with you helped me greatly in building my self-esteem and in dealing with a relationship issue I couldn't let go of. I highly recommend you for your professionalism, listening skills, and support during difficult and complex processes..."

"Starting therapy gave me a different perspective on life, thanks to your knowledge, your professionalism, and your personal approach and way of talking about your own life. It's clear you're consistent. I came to your space out of desperation, as a last resort, without realizing how much I needed to get to know myself, to build and deconstruct. Today I can say that I am myself, that I know where I'm going because I have confidence and self-esteem. And while I consider this a personal achievement, it largely has to do with you…"

"I think your space is one of comfort, convenience, and safety when you share what you're going through and feeling. That freed me up a lot..."

"The experience was very positive in terms of seeing life differently. And knowing that there are no limits to achieving what you truly want in life. Pursuing dreams and knowing that those dreams, which we often see as impossible,

made me see that they are actually achievable. And that we can achieve them by having certain habits, focusing on them, and being positive. Because most of the time we see our dreams as unattainable, it's actually us who put up barriers for ourselves. Your perspective as a therapist was very interesting to me because you showed me that everything is achievable with planning, perseverance, and optimism. And that it's also possible to redesign and choose again..."

"Therapy helped me settle down and make certain decisions that benefited me both professionally and socially. That was very important for me..."

"With you, I learned when it comes to human relationships, to have a greater degree of tolerance and patience with certain situations. And also to have the courage to set certain boundaries that I didn't set before. So that my personal space and development aren't invaded. And to see that relationships are also a space for personal growth and projection. To be able to better manage my freedom and feel happier."

Here are testimonies from some female patients:

"For me, space is liberating. Valuable. I feel heard and understood. It helps me become a better person. Someone I am incredibly grateful to for transforming my life, day by day, for the better..."

"I felt contained. Understood. Relieved. Clear on future actions. Reset...
"*

"Welcoming and healing. Transformative. I feel like it saved me. Self-esteem booster. A system reset, a reconnection with "my true self." Comforting, educational, and there was no shortage of good humor..."

"Doing psychotherapy with you opened my mind and helped me see problems from a different perspective. What seemed like a dead end, I realized I was able to get out..."

"Forever grateful would be my way of describing my experience with you for everything you helped me discover about my past and how you helped me sustain myself to move forward…"

"A safe space to show myself as I am. I discovered a ton of tools I needed and still use to this day. You're empathetic and loving…"

"I never felt judged. Something I feared because of previous traumatic experiences with your colleagues. Thanks to you, I redefined the space and realized that only I can recognize the value within me…"

"An experience of growth, transformation, expansion, and above all, empowerment…"

"It gave me the tools to face my challenges with strength and move forward. It rescued me from myself and helped me find a way to navigate my journeys with confidence…"

"With you, I made the most important and wise decision. To quit my job as a sales clerk and open my beauty salon, which is still going strong 10 years ago. To leave with the feeling that everything will be okay and to feel at peace…"

"My experience with you was like a shining light that illuminated the completely dark path I was on. Very positive, and your patient care is excellent…"

"Totally positive and healing, where I learned and continue to learn to love myself first, in order to love others…"

"My own space to expand and generate my absolute power..."

"It was an internal growth, several discoveries, and the realization that you can always overcome difficult situations. You helped me take the step of seeing what I couldn't see in myself. I opened a huge door that keeps opening wider..."

"It's hard to describe in a few words what you mean to me. You're my subconscious that I don't want to listen to, my guide and my support..."

"My ex-partner and I only went once; he didn't want to go anymore. But you were kind, attentive, listened to us, and were eager to work. So thank you for that..."

"Totally positive and healing, where I learned and continue to learn to love myself first, in order to love others..."

"Liberating. You helped me make decisions. Constructive. From imbalance to virtuous transformation. I would say "no return," it only depends on you and your choices..."

"I would use a very short phrase, but it makes a lot of sense to me. The therapy was: At the right time..."

"A system reboot, a reunion with my true self..."

"My experience with you was the best, I would always recommend you. Beautiful inside and out, and an excellent professional..."

"You have a capacity for listening and empathy, especially with older adults, and extraordinary patience, but also an uncommon acuity and a capacity

for interventions that don't let anything that emerges escape you. It's not very common. These aren't qualities that everyone possesses. With you, I've completed a cycle of two previous analysts with extensive experience..."

"Forever grateful would be my way of describing my experience with you for everything you helped me discover about my past and how you helped me sustain myself to move forward..."

"You helped me and continue to help me navigate life in harmony, first with myself and then with others..."

"I would say disruptive..."

"You made me see the value I had within me. I was able to step out of my comfort zone, stop having silly fears that don't exist, give myself the value I deserve, distance myself from people who don't add up, stop stressing about things outside of me..."

"Every day you become more beautiful and full of light. You are unfor-gettable to me. Your words are always so precise. I grew with you. I learned to love myself. You are in my heart. Thank you..."

"The path to saving and finding myself, recognizing that shining is good, and if anyone is dazzled, kisses and thank you very much..."

"I just want to say thank you. You helped me regain my self-confidence. After each session, I always feel calm and empowered. You're the best! I don't usually recommend anyone, but I always recommend you. And I'm sending you this message from Ezeiza International Airport, on my way to Berlin. What more could you possibly want? Big kisses..."

"Tranquility, love, peace. I know it's not a prayer or a phrase, but it's what I always felt in our space..."

"Excellent active listening skills, empathy, and intuitive handling. Timely and accurate interventions that helped promote necessary and/or desired changes in me. Constantly updated and trained..."

"Accept our darkness and from there begin the change..."

"I'm truly forever grateful for having found you. So many beautiful things to say. You changed my life for the better; you helped me see myself through different eyes and learn to love and value myself. Your energy and light were refreshing. And I love you so much. You'll always be the best recommendation I can give!"

"You did me a great service! You were the one who held the mirror up so I could look at myself again and find myself!"

"Gratitude and infinite love to the one who helped me transcend my anger and sadness, filling it with light and so much love, tenderness, and understanding. I adore you..."

"You taught me to love the plot more than the outcome. You are the fairy godmother of empowerment..."

"You motivated me to be encouraged, to undertake, to train myself and grow. To become more and more myself..."

"The space was a constant learning experience, a journey of trusting myself and believing that I can always shine..."

"Peacemaker, I made access bars to consciousness with you and it changed me for the better..."

"You helped me wake up, to value myself, to rebuild that part of me I thought had been destroyed. You are pure magic..."

"You give the profession a twist. You take it out of the classic format and rebuild your own path. It's like you find with a different space. With all the potential. And sometimes we think so small that we don't dare to see all that can be achieved and unfolded. Thank you for that."

"Trust me to trust others. As you say; you go fast alone, far in a network. I want to be part of your network, and you part of mine..."

"An extremely positive experience. I found empathy, a professional approach in the discussions, and a chance to discover myself; through challenges, discomfort, and interventions, I learned that I built my world from my self-love..."

"It allowed me to clarify and rethink aspects of myself that were holding me back..."

"Through psychotherapy with you, I can be myself and show who I am, and even on a bad day, walk away with a smile, saying: I can do this and more..."

"Transformative, realistic, and healing. A before and after..."

"The space is intense and profound. Moments of reflection where I recognize the ability to break my own limits. You are always ready and available

in presence and distance..."

"You're by far the best. I learned that what others think says more about them than about us. We judge by our standards! Who are we to judge? I understood it's a process, and I choose the word TRUST. I understood that we can't control anything, that everything flows, and that's liberating. I stopped demanding so much of myself and allowed myself to feel my emotions and manage them without dwelling on them. You're generous and the kindest..."

Inspiration Exercise

Create your own Playlist

• Select songs that cheer you up and fill you with positive energy. Include both your favorites and some with inspiring lyrics. Listen to this playlist whenever you need a boost.

Story Game

• Invite some friends or family members to the game. Each person shares a personal anecdote that's inspirational, motivational, or funny. You can even assign themes like "overcoming challenges" or "moments of unexpected happiness."

Create your Dream Map

• With old magazines, printouts, scissors, and glue, spend some time cutting out images and words that represent your dreams and aspirations. Glue everything onto a large piece of cardboard to create your own "Dream Map." Place it somewhere visible to remind yourself of your goals and keep you motivated.

Write a letter

• Directed to your future self. Describe Your current dreams, your accomplishments, and what you hope to have achieved in the next five years. Seal the letter and keep it in a safe place to open on the date you've written on the envelope.

Photo shoot

• Organize a themed photo shoot for yourself or with friends. Choose an original theme, such as "superheroes," "space travel," or "retro 80s." Dress accordingly and take creative photos. This exercise not only inspires you, but also takes you away from the drama and provides fun memories to share.

Micro adventures

• Plan small, spontaneous adventures. It could be a bike ride to a new place, a picnic in the park, a karaoke night at home, or a day exploring interesting places in a city you've never been to.

THANK YOURSELF: And If your story inspired someone and transformed their life, thank you. Thank you, if instead of being indifferent you turned your gaze to someone who needed it, who waited for you because you went to meet the world being you. Do not judge yourself confident or naïve. Everyone gives what he has. Those who cannot appreciate it, will miss it. Follow being you. Thank you for your falls, thank you for holding the ground tight to propel yourself forward. Be grateful for your tears, your despair, be grateful for the frustration that moved you from that place that wasn't meant for you. Be grateful for the hugs you received. Be grateful for the opportunities that manage. Be grateful for your breath. Be grateful for your patience. Be grateful for your power. Be grateful for your will to live.

Be thankful for everything and everyone. There are no mistakes. Your story is the one you were meant to live – even if it seems cruel – even if it hurts – even if you don't fully understand today. I promise you, there are hidden blessings.

ASK: When I chose my profession at 13, I never imagined how many lives I would impact. I just listened to something inside me that whispered, "Psychology." At the time, I wasn't fully aware of the depth of what I would learn or the human commitment it entailed. Today, after 20 years of practice, I can say with certainty that I was born to do this.

Along my journey, I've discovered that everything we align ourselves with controls us, but we're also controlled by what we resist and reject. Whenever we use energy to sustain or fight something, we remain trapped in its influence.

Consciousness, in its true essence, never creates separation; on the contrary, it generates oneness. If what we call consciousness leads us to distance ourselves from others, to feel superior, or to differentiate, then it is not consciousness. We are operating from another place, the ego. In consciousness, everything is included.

And if there is something in us that cannot receive this truth, would you be willing to let it go?

One tool I've shared with my patients is the power of the "interesting point of view." This doesn't simply mean saying, "How interesting that you have that point of view and I have another." It's about adopting a genuinely curious perspective, being willing to see from a different angle what, from our perspective, we might not be able to understand.

When you don't align yourself with or buy into an idea, but you don't reject it either, you resist, you simply are. That's where the possibility of infinite choice exists.

ANSWER: _____

_____

_____

_____

_____

_____

KEY TRUTH: "The quality of your relationships with the outside world reflects the quality of the relationship you have with yourself, within."

In a created world to being a hero is an act of profound self-love. We are heroines in a world made for heroes.

A transformative woman is a woman who allows herself to be transformed.

The burden of being a hero is a heavy one for someone who only wants to live in freedom and happy with themselves. Encourage yourself to run away from that stereotypical place and let yourself be surprised by someone who is willing to see you beyond a stigmatizing pattern.

Men and women complement each other, and we should never lose sight of the fact that both energies are required for life to continue. There are no better or worse. We shouldn't seek to confront each other. I don't believe in the separation of powers, nor in the extremes of feminism and machismo. This tension that we have experienced for centuries is due to a system that proclaims "divide and conquer."

Being and contributing to an energy that is natural to you as a living being (male or female) is the best and greatest choice you can make for your existence

These exercises seek to ignite your creativity and joy, turning every moment into an opportunity to inspire and be inspired.

Have fun and let your light shine!

Chapter 6: Silence

They realized that it is full of public speaking courses, but no one is willing to listen. Inhabiting silence is uncomfortable and that is where growth lies.

The healing power of silence and meaningful words – how to accept and communicate our own truth.

Internal validation, signs for your next adventure

There comes a time in life when, without needing anyone to confirm it, you simply know you're ready for what's next. Not because someone tells you so, not because you've met certain external requirements, but because you feel it in your body. And you can trust that validation.

Believing in the voice of your spirit, in the guidance of your heart, trusting the energy of your essence, is what shows you all these signs to know what to say, where to go, who to be with. You don't need to cling to the apparent security of a family structure, a country, or your comfort zone. True security is born in your being, in connection with your own truth, with your essence, with that inner strength that gives you the courage to live more fully.

It's almost like a revelation that comes without anyone having to explain it. One day you realize it's time. The next event is just around the corner; the unknown is knocking at your door; a new level of consciousness is calling out to you. And you don't quite know what's happening, but you move forward. Contraction, expansion, every moment of your choices is necessary for what we call growth. Both energies coexist when a quantum leap is taking place.

I remember when I was 17, just finishing high school, my family was restructuring, and the grief was still ongoing. Yet, my whole being clearly showed me what was next – excited, with the adrenaline of the unknown. I decided to move to Rosario in Argentina, a much larger city than the one I'd lived in throughout my childhood and adolescence. It was home to one of the most prestigious psychology schools in my country, a pioneer in the field. I was going to going to be on my own and would have to deal with my strengths and weaknesses. Because when you're conscious, neither impossibilities, nor fears, nor grief can hold you back.

A year ago, the same process of contraction – expansion happened to me in which my whole being indicated my motion. This time, the destination would be the other side of the globe, literally – North America.

I've always believed that our destiny is never a place, but a new perspective – a different way of perceiving reality and dealing with it, of making ourselves uncomfortable, of stretching our structures until we finally perceive the infinite possibilities available.

I constantly celebrate each amplitude, receiving what comes and connecting with that frequency, moving whatever is required to reach a new space of consciousness.

And be careful that when I say contraction I do not associate it with something negative and expansion, with its opposite positive. Nothing is right or wrong. These are merely definitions of the rational, cognitive mind. Contraction and expansion are instances that you require for growth because you are alive and in constant dynamic change. It's like your heart, lungs, or stomach expanding and contracting, and in that dialectic lies vitality.

To contract is to return to your interior to review where you are now, what your being requires, and where you need to refocus.

Expansion is going out into the world to share your gifts, to be an invitation, to see diverse people arrive and to observe how everything you moved inside is expressed outside,

As it is within, so it is without.

And what you discover within, you will inevitably reflect in your creations, in the opportunities you attract to yourself, in the life you ultimately lead. You chose to build. It's just a matter of listening to yourself and taking the next step.

The magic of inhabiting silence

We live in a world obsessed with talking. There are public speaking courses on every corner; manuals on how to express yourself better; techniques to persuade and convince. But who is truly willing to listen? Who stops to inhabit the discomfort of silence?

Growth is not only in the words spoken, but also in the pause between one idea and another. In the void we leave when we don't compulsively fill every moment with conclusions or noise, there is an opportunity to listen.

We've been taught to speak, but not to listen, much less to listen to ourselves or our intuition, to our body and its manifestations. And, in turn, communicating isn't necessarily understanding. Imagine the complexity of connecting. We are beings who don't know ourselves, trying to connect with others who also don't know who they are.

Understanding oneself and others is made possible by non-cognitive, non-rational, non-theoretical knowledge. Understanding is a conscious experience. It takes some people a lifetime to develop healthy relationships. And some don't even achieve it. I have seen very young children be extraordinarily understanding of everything the universe around them and manifest their inner world with total clarity.

Understanding has nothing to do with education, intellect, or age, nor with psycho-emotional maturity. It's something we're born with, which we later erase through exposure to culture, indoctrination, and impositions.

This is how social and family mandates operate within us and block us. The rational mind dictates our daily lives, and we become fragmented, diminished, and dissociated from our knowledge, from listening, from perceiving, and from receiving the blessings bestowed upon us throughout our lives. We forget who we are.

The word and its power

Words have a profound impact on our psychic reality. The "human cub" becomes a subject thanks to language upon its entry into culture, according to Sigmund Freud, a Viennese neurologist who discovered that the human mind is governed by a deeper, more ancient structure called the unconscious, thus configuring what we call the symbolic instance.

Our unconscious is pure signifier, stated Jacques Lacan, a French analyst who rewrote Freud's theory. The unconscious is not a repository of repressed ideas, but a system of signifiers – words, symbols, and discursive structures – that governs our subjectivity. That is, what we call "unconscious desire," does not arise as a pure biological impulse, but as an effect of language itself. Our traumas, dreams, and symptoms are expressed following rules similar to those of language with metaphors, displacements, and wordplay.

When we speak, we are not completely in control of our speech, because the unconscious *already speaks through us.*

Therefore, psychoanalysis is developed through a process of deep listening, where failures, lapses, and repetitions can reveal the person's repressed desires and articulate a singular truth not recognized by the speaker.

Imagine the importance of words in our entire lives. They not only express thoughts, but shape our entire reality, making our desires and feelings tangible. They bring them to the world.

Learning to speak is one of the first biological learnings we have in childhood, but achieving communication can take a lifetime. Communicating is permeated by that unknown truth of the subject and implies an act of courage; undress before the other without embellishments or masks. And that is not at all simple.

Even if we believe ourselves to be authentic, absolutely all of us go to the social encounter with what I call "a character" who, like a the pilot on a rainy day, protects the intimidating truth that makes us human subjects.

Do you say everything?

Be honest, with yourself, not with me. I'm sure that in the shadows of your intimacy there are truths that you don't dare to reveal or confess to anyone or even your pillow. And that's okay. You don't have to do it – just acknowledge it.

Recognizing ourselves, seeing ourselves in those places we hate about ourselves and are ashamed of, is not at all easy to express.

I have noticed a little because of my profession, and listen. I've talked to so many people in 20 years that sometimes they choose to speak without really knowing what they want to communicate. They're afraid to reveal themselves.

This happens only in our species. And it happens because human language has that particular characteristic of "telling and hiding at the same time."

That is to say, when we speak, we never say what we truly mean. Language, while communicating, also conceals. In the animal kingdom, language is simple and authentic. Humans, on the other hand, fill the conversation with borrowed rhetoric, clichés, what we think others want to hear, what we think they need from us.

How often do we communicate who we truly are? How often do we allow ourselves the vulnerability of a genuine word?

Accepting and communicating our own truth requires courage and isn't easy, but it's certainly less exhausting than maintaining the disguise we wear every day for a lifetime.

The only reason we don't do it is for fear of being judged, feeling ridiculous, or not being accepted. And so we fragment ourselves from our wholeness and mutate ourselves to satisfy ideas we believe are vital, which ultimately no one cares about.

You need, first, to learn to connect with your knowledge, validate that truth, allow yourself all kinds of opinions, judgments, and criticisms to finally accept yourself as the infinite being that you are.

And this is where silence and calm take on real value. Only in this space can we inhabit us without interference.

Silence, a challenge and an opportunity

Silence makes us uncomfortable because it confronts us with what we avoid – those fissures in us that we don't want to acknowledge. It shows us everything we don't want to reveal because it shows us the excuses – the lack of commitment, the inaction, the wounds, the selfishness, and the damage we've caused ourselves.

That's why we fill it with empty words, with noise, with distractions like, "I'm afraid, I feel guilty, I won't be able to do it."

Daring to inhabit it is finally letting go of the disguise, the mask we created long ago in adolescence to "be part" of a family, a social group, a culture. Listening to silence offers us the possibility of finding the answers we don't want to see because they challenge us, they make us uncomfortable.

Silence is your patient teacher. It shows you that not everything needs to be said, that not everything needs to be explained or justified. It gives you the opportunity to choose your words with empathy, rather than reacting impulsively. It allows you to observe without judgment, to feel before responding.

All of life's lessons, you'll see if you learn!

Every conversation, every silence, and every written word brings us to a moment of greater awareness. But the consciousness doesn't arise from definitions, stigmatizations, or dogmatic discourses. Consciousness is, by definition, light, natural, and automatic.

So, I wonder: *Would you be willing to learn about your truth and stop making excuses for not being?*

When we speak from our authentic selves, when we listen to ourselves with true presence and allow ourselves that uncomfortable space of silence, communication transforms beautifully; it feels magical.

Our receiving expands, and our being opens up. It's no longer just about speaking, but about connecting. It's no longer just about speaking, but about healing.

Living in silence and using words consciously gives us immense power – the power to choose what we create in our lives and how we significantly impact the lives of others.

Maybe it's time to stop worrying about speaking well and start learning to truly listen – with your heart.

What are you choosing to communicate today? From what position are you speaking and listening?

Lulu, an unexpected teacher

Silence has immense value. In it, the mind quiets and the heart speaks. It is in this space that genuine observation flourishes: seeing without judging, listening without interpreting, feeling without rushing. It is there that we connect with a deeper language – one that emerges from the soul, without the rigidity of reason.

My daughter, Lulu, gives me this divine wisdom with her mere presence. She lives from the essence of being, with genuine love and an extraordinary existential joy, which doesn't require over-interpretations.

Her gaze is without judgment, free of pretensions, over-interpretations and transparent. She reminds me at every step what really matters in life – human connection without masks or conditions.

Thirteen years ago I chose motherhood. It wasn't an easy path, but it was one of much learning and a complete transformation of myself. She became my teacher. She showed me that her condition isn't a limitation, but rather an expression of human biodiversity.

Seeing beyond her extra chromosome, taught me to open myself to a new way of understanding life, where perfection isn't found in what fits certain imposed molds, but in what overflows with love.

Being her mother has been and is the most powerful experience I've had up to this point. I don't think anyone can even imagine the challenges that this motherhood entails.

Lulu belongs to that universe called the Down syndrome community. It's a very happy universe, with enormous warmth and social power. These people have a desire to show the world who they are and a tremendous desire to do things.

If you are expecting the arrival of a baby with Down syndrome, I know what you're going through – the voices in your head, the anxiety, and the fear for the future.

The fear of the unknown is natural; I understand. But before judging it as something negative, I invite you to allow yourself to recognize the differences that inhabit the world. And at the same time, know that you are not alone. There is a community ready to support you, to lend a hand, and to show you that, although the path is unique, it is full of light.

I also want to tell you that there's a limit to neurosis that you'll have to learn to manage if you want to lead your child's life in a healthy way. Because, truly, today I realize this happens to all of us. Or does it?

Think about this, if you are in charge and try to mold a person as you wish, and achieve it, what do you think could happen? Most likely, that person will go crazy. As I always say, the other (son, brother, stranger) is another person.

So there is a place where, as parents we must be able to recognize that our child as another, and stop doing with them what we consider best. And simply encourage them to be the best they can be, with their potential and limitations, in a context of fulfilling themselves as people.

This is basically for all children, whether they have a condition or not. In other words, we must redefine that being as a human person in a family and social context.

Science still calls them "chromosomal errors." I know that nature doesn't make mistakes. These beings arrive with a purpose: to awaken in us the capacity to love unconditionally, to communicate without words, and to celebrate life in its purest form.

If you are willing to welcome them, I assure you they will transform your existence for the better – and forever.

When we dare to take charge of our lives and our being, we not only create our dreams and transform ourselves dynamically, but we also inspire others in their own process of change.

The way you connect with yourself is the same way you connect with others, and from there, you make an impact. The key to communicating authentically is to start with yourself – with that inner voice that needs to be heard before you can express yourself with intention.

In this process, stopping to think about what others want or expect to hear is to nullify yourself subjectively, seeking acceptance or validation from others.

We are all lost stars trying to illuminate the darkness. We are born with gifts that deserve to be explored and then shared. Focusing on what the universe around you wants to hear is entering its perspective, and with it, diminish you, limit your natural human potential and block your true essence.

In a world where few dare to *simply* be themselves, authenticity makes the difference. Go ahead, go for it, you can inspire many more people to the transformations they truly need.

Exercise of Silence: Connecting with Your Being

Silence isn't empty – it's the space where we can truly listen to ourselves. In a world saturated with noise, finding moments of silence allows us to access deep clarity and expand our consciousness.

1. Find a quiet space

Where you won't be interrupted. It could be your home, nature, or any place where you feel calm.

2. Adopt a comfortable position

Sitting comfortably or with your back on the floor, lying down, if you wish you prefer. The important thing is that your body is relaxed, present, and calm.

3. Close your eyes and breathe deeply

Inhale through your nose in four counts, hold your breath for a few seconds and exhale slowly through your mouth. Repeat this process several times until your body feels completely relaxed.

4. Observe the silence

Don't try fill it with thoughts. I only perceived the space, the sound of the environment, your breathing. If thoughts appear, they will surely be so, just observe them without getting hooked in them. Don't try to stop them.

5. Ask yourself a question and listen

In this state of calm, ask the following question:

What do I truly know that I'm not yet acknowledging? What is true for me right now? If I were to let go of all judgments and expectations, what would that create in my life?

6. Permit the answers to emerge

Don't force them. Just stay present and receptive. Sometimes, the answer won't come in words, but in sensations, images, or intuitions.

7. Give thanks and return slowly

After a few minutes, bring awareness back to your body, move your fingers gently and opened your eyes.

8. Write down your impressions

If you wish, write down what you felt, thought, or perceived.

Benefits of this exercise:

✓ Greater mental clarity
✓ Connection with your intuition
✓ Reduction of anxiety and stress
✓ Expansion of consciousness and creativity

Exercise for Assertive Communication

Assertive communication allows us to express what we feel, think, and need clearly and respectfully, without attacking or subjugating others. This exercise helps you strengthen your ability to express yourself with confidence and empathy.

1. Connect with your intention

Before you speak, ask yourself: *What message do I really want to convey? What emotion am I communicating from: fear, anger, calm, or clarity? Is my intention to create chaos or to react?*

Example: When you are angry, instead of letting it dominate you, acknowledge the emotion and drop an expression of serenity. "Yes to everything as it is." Just conscious observation.

2. Use this assertive communication model (or one you prefer):

• Express how you feel ☛ "I feel..."

• Describe the situation without judgment ☛ "When it happens..."

• Explain why it affects you ☛ "Because to me it means..."

• Propose a solution or express your need ☛ "I would like..."

Example: Instead of saying, "You never listen to me. You always do what you want."

Try saying, "I feel ignored when you don't take my opinion into account in our decisions. It's important to me to feel like my voice counts, too. I'd like us to be able to find a solution together."

3. Practice active listening

Communication isn't just about speaking, it's also about listening with presence. Practice:

  • Look the person in the eyes

  • No interruptions

  • Validate what is said: "I understand this is important to you."

  • Clarifying question: "How would you like to solve it?"

4. Adjust your tone and body language

  • Keep an open and relaxed posture

  • Speak with a firm but kind tone

  • Avoid crossing your arms or making impatient gestures.

5. Reflect after the conversation

Did I manage to express what I wanted without aggression or submission? Did I truly listen to the other person? How can I improve my communication next time?

Benefits of this exercise:

  ✓ It helps you express what you think without fear
  ✓ Improve your personal and professional relationships
  ✓ Increase your confidence and clarity when speaking
  ✓ Reduces conflicts and misunderstandings

Assertive communication is a skill that grows stronger with practice. The more conscious you are of how you express yourself, the more positive impact you'll have on others and on your own life.

Silence is a portal. Dare to inhabit it and discover what it has to show you.

THANK YOURSELF: I take this moment to thank me deeply for allowing me the space I needed to inhabit silence and listen to my truth. Thanks to this, I am able to validate the richness of my being and the wisdom that resides in the depths of my soul.

Thank you for having the courage to disconnect from the noise of the outside world, even though it may lead to judgment. Thank you for allowing me pause and silence, where I find clarity and possibilities. Thank you for trusting my intuition and embracing my authenticity without fear.

I realize that by listening to myself, I'm building a more fulfilling and dynamically meaningful life. I'm grateful for my commitment to myself and my ability to continue growing and learning.

ASK: Are you willing to learn about your truth and stop making excuses for not being? What are you choosing to communicate today? From what place are you speaking and listening? What are you choosing to believe today? Are you going to nourish your being with possibilities and expansion? Or will you continue compulsively consuming the toxicity of the world, allowing it to poison you effortlessly? From where are you choosing to create your future?

ANSWER: _____

_____

_____

_____

_____

_____

KEY TRUTH: Everyone wants to talk, but very few know how to listen. Silence is uncomfortable because it reveals what we keep quiet. True growth lies in that pause. Words only heal when they are born of truth.

Who speaks without consciousness, it just makes noise.

Who is listening, is transformed. Life whispers lessons to us at every moment. You decide whether to ignore them or learn from them.

Chapter 7: Dissatisfaction

If someone gave you a box with everything you've lost in life, what would be the first thing you would look for?

Longing for what I don't have; despising what is there; the eternal nonconformity of being human.

Never before in human history have, we had so many options, so many possible paths, so much information available, and so quickly.

However, so why do we feel such a powerful existential void? Why do we continue to experience this constant dissatisfaction, this internal noise that never stops even when everything on the outside seems "right"?

We live surrounded by stimuli, voices, opinions, quick fixes, and formulas for success. And we are so out of touch with what's essential.

A genuine connection with others – especially with ourselves – has become scarce or nonexistent. We move through life as if everything were urgent, something that happened yesterday, without giving ourselves permission to stop, look within, and recognize what we are truly feeling or what we desire. Observation devoid of urgency, connection without control or expectations, seem like utopian ideals.

We don't give ourselves the space of kindness to enjoy living.

What the Italians call "la dolce far niente" means "the sweetness of doing nothing" or "the pleasure of idleness."

An expression that highlights the importance of enjoying rest and tranquility in life, without the need to be constantly busy or productive. It emphasizes the beauty and pleasure that can be found in the simple act of doing nothing.

Enjoy the present moment, in solitude or with someone significant; it's a great invitation for us Westerners. It's a call to relax and appreciate the little things in life, without the need to always think about the future or pending tasks.

"Dolce far niente" is not just a phrase; it's a philosophy of life that values rest, calm, and tranquility as essential parts of good human living.

Everywhere you look, you see people yearning for what they don't have, obsessing over what they're "missing," clearly referring to "things or status." Running around, stressed, oblivious to their own choices, fantasizing about other people's lives while they ignore or despise their own, what has already been granted to them, what truly exists. And so, from that absence of presence, of gratitude, of genuine appreciation, they make decisions that distance themselves even further from themselves.

The root of dissatisfaction isn't in what's missing, but in a lack of presence with what you truly already have; in not inhabiting the moment; in not recognizing what already is.

Thus, we create paths from a place of scarcity, not from awareness. We choose from the confusion of haste, rather than from the clarity of serenity. We follow steps imposed by others, hoping to find answers that can truly only come from the depths of our being.

What would happen if we gave ourselves permission to create a different path?

A path where the goal isn't to fill a void, but to inhabit who we are. One where the here and now isn't an obstacle, but the starting point. One where recognizing who we already are is the true revolutionary act. And where what we have is a matter of absolute gratitude.

Perhaps the new path is not built by moving faster but stopping us.

Breathing. Listening. Returning to the body. Instantly. To the inner truth. And from there, from that place where nothing is missing, where everything is, we can simply begin.

For now, we are still overly inundated with information based on fixed points of view and rigid definitions. Science, for example, builds certainty and predictable models. The same is true of artificial intelligence; it processes pre-existing information and generates results based on patterns and probabilities.

What if we stopped operating from the predictable and entered into the awareness of multiple possibilities?

Here, quantum physics has everything to contribute; offering us a perspective of the future that is no longer a straight line, because anything can change in an instant. A single different choice can transform your entire reality, shattering any predictions based on algorithms. In a state of consciousness expanded, we become an explosion of possibilities. In contrast, when we operate from a purely Newtonian perspective, we are tied to repetition, to fixed structures easily replicated by AI. There is no creation, only imitation.

So, where will you continue choosing to create your future today?

If you limit yourself to what is known, to what is established, your life is going to be very predictable. If you open to new possibilities, you enter a space where everything can change at any moment. And that's where true transformation happens.

STATISTICS:

Worldwide, two-thirds of the 8 billion people living on this planet will die from preventable diseases. Approximately 13 percent of all deaths worldwide are attributed to diseases affecting the heart and circulation: heart disease, stroke, chronic respiratory diseases, cancer, and finally diabetes. Nearly 400 million young children have suffered or suffer some form of violence in their homes. Nine percent of the world's population is malnourished. 149 million children under 5 years of age are stunted as a result. An estimated 582 million people will live with chronic malnutrition in the coming years. One in three women is a victim of physical or sexual violence at some point in her life. On average, men have a higher mortality rate than women. The causes vary. But life expectancy in wealthy countries for men is 76 to 78; for women it is 81 to 83. And in the Americas, for the first time this century, life expectancy is declining dramatically. [1]

How do we change this? **Choosing.**

BECAUSE IT'S NO LONGER JUST ABOUT PREVENTING ILLNESS OR DEATH, BUT ABOUT LEARNING TO LIVE LIFE.

In the vastness of our existence, we fall into a subtle and profound cycle, yearning for what we don't have and despising what we do have. It's an almost invisible trap. It robs us of the present, strips us of our ability to appreciate the beauty of everyday life. We are insatiable dreamers, always searching for what seems beyond, while ignoring the miracle that already dwells in what is close, what is true, what is here.

We're bombarded by images of perfect lives, other people's achievements, and unattainable goals. Social media shows us an edited happiness, a cosmetic existence that makes us feel inadequate. Thus, we fall into the trap of comparison, believing that happiness lies in what we don't have, instead of recognizing it in who we already are.

This constant comparison leads to chronic dissatisfaction. We feel incomplete, as if something else is always missing. This feeling erodes mental health, fueling anxiety, sadness, envy, depression, and suicide. It also hurts our relationships: it distances us from those we love, because it makes us feel more or less; never equal, never truly connected.

Is there an antidote? Well, for me, it does exist. At least it's worked for me in times of great darkness and despair. It's called gratitude.

Being grateful brings us back to the present. It teaches us to see what already exists, to value what has already been gained, to find beauty even in what is broken. Gratitude doesn't negate the desire to move forward, but rather anchors it to a solid foundation. It reminds us that not all is lost – that not all is insufficient – that we are already abundant in many wonderful ways.

From my perspective, true happiness lies in that subtle balance between wanting more and appreciating who we already are. It's a dance between our life's expectations and gratitude for everything that happens. There are no magic formulas, just practice, observation, and self-compassion.

I've always been intrigued by the confusion our psyche creates, the awareness that there's something more, not outside, but waiting to emerge within. I've experienced, felt, and witnessed the desire for something that wasn't in my life, without appreciating what I already had. And then, when things changed – by choice or by fate – I was able to appreciate the value of what I hadn't been able to see at the time.

IF TODAY I HAD THE POWER TO SEARCH FOR WHAT I FEEL I LOST AT SOME POINT IN MY LIFE, IN THAT MAGIC BOX OF LOST AND FOUND, I THINK I WOULD GO STRAIGHT TO MY INNOCENCE. THAT NAIVETÉ WITH WHICH I OBSERVED THE WORLD AS A CHILD, THAT NATURAL ABILITY TO CONNECT WITH THE JOY OF LIFE, TO BE SURPRISED BY EVERYTHING AND ENJOY EVERY EXPERIENCE.

Growing up hardens you, it distances you from the emotional world; you stop playing, dreaming, loving. And little by little, almost without realizing it, you also stop living. You just go on automatic.

Resilience is remembering. It's feeling again. It's being a phoenix; turning from ashes to be reborn. It's not about having everything under control, but about seeking balance, even in chaos. About finding beauty amidst the storms. Resilience teaches us that it is possible to survive, and it is also possible to transform. And that every transformation can be born from the simplest thing – a choice.

It's the possibility of making a dream come true that makes life interesting. Dreams sustain us, propel us, give us direction. And when you raise your standards, the universe responds. Not because it rewards, but because it reflects. The universe doesn't demand sacrifices; the universe creates miracles. And when your actions align with your desires, everything magically flows.

The human mind is full of contradictions. But amidst this enigma, there is one certainty that can guide us: learn to value the present, to be grateful for what we already are; and never stop dreaming. Embrace our innocence. Honor our resilience. Choose to make our wishes come true. That is true alchemy.

A great life is possible only when we take responsibility, in all areas. If we leave it in the hands of others, we condemn ourselves to dissatisfaction. And dissatisfied people, do you know what they do? They consume networks, social patterns, compulsive shopping, superficial connections, and everything we observe on a daily basis.

When we believe the solution lies outside, we also find culprits there: I don't have money, it's this country and its crises, it's the politicians, it's my partner who no longer looks after me, it's my children who exhaust me, it's my boss who always demands more, and an endless list of culprits, without taking responsibility.

However, by recognizing that everything is inside, within us that we create so?

The life you have is the life you choose. You created it. Whether you accept it or not. Whether you're aware of it or deny it and blame it on any circumstance. You did it to make yourself more aware.

Being conscious will give you the opportunity to decide whether this life you're living is still joyful for you, or if it's time to transform it. And accepting this will involve making decisions that may involve uncomfortable conversations or difficult actions. That's why the vast majority of people in the world, responsible for their own unhappiness avoid choosing to avoid discomfort.

Being vulnerable is being present with what you're experiencing and recognizing that you are the creator of your reality, over and over again. Even if the reality you're choosing may be completely unhealthy. It's unleashing your abilities without falling into victimhood. It's working on your self-love, your confidence, and your ability to choose, as many times as necessary, to create what you desire – with individual commitment and empathy for others.

Because, to be completely honest, the greatest enemy of possibilities is our limiting beliefs. And we create our reality 100 percent based on them. Your mind is fertile ground. What you sow there defines what you will reap in your life. So, focus on what ideas, thoughts, and beliefs you decide to incorporate because without coherence in your being, focus and constant action, your dreams won't happen.

A Different Vision

My therapeutic goal has always been to address anxiety, and the full range of symptoms it encompasses, as a potential by taking an integrative approach to health through individual empowerment, including being in a broader social context than their own internal world.

Our environment greatly influences our pathological processes. This is what is known as epigenetics, that is, how the environment, our emotions, diet, thoughts, and experiences can influence the way our genes express themselves, without changing the DNA itself.

It's as if DNA were a book with instructions, and epigenetics decides which chapters are read and which aren't, based on what we experience. Or, even more interestingly, what we choose to experience.

What's significantly valuable about the discoveries of scientific observation is that it's proven that we can influence our genetics through our choices and the environment we create for ourselves, as well as through the way our eye, as an observer, looks.

Recognizing our greatest strengths in vulnerability, creating a unique and unformatted approach that adapts to each person's unique needs, is how I have approached the clinic since my inception.

My focus is on an extraterritorial approach that transcends the traditional boundaries of patient care. A space where everyone can find the anchor and bridge they need to thrive because mental well-being knows no borders.

This distinctive and adaptable model values individuality and departs from conventional methods. It promotes a global, inclusive, and transformative vision of people's well-being today.

In this social context, each once again, in this challenging time, many people experience anxiety and difficulties with their mental and physical health. They feel disoriented, affected, unmotivated, and without the tools to manage their emotions or find meaningful support. Generic solutions don't solve any of their problems. On the contrary, they leave them further trapped in a spiral of isolation and hopelessness, which is extremely depressing. And compulsive or distracting consumption is a favorable opportunity to further damage our capacity for choice and healthy living. I have observed the dynamic and successful metamorphosis of many people who have decided to take responsibility for their own existence.

It is that we still live in a world directed and governed mostly by monarchical powers as in past centuries, which dictate how we should live. Starting your own life project is giving yourself the opportunity to create it as you like, not taking you from the system, but not submitting to it either. It's about being attentive to what works for you, in all areas of your life. And that requires constant presence and choice.

It's time to embrace this new paradigm and expand it generatively, of offering real answers to real needs, of fostering a genuine openness to reality and daring to transform it.

Many of us have been inspired by a more conscious archetype of choices as a reflection of each of our lives.

An integrative approach to the health and life of people is my contribution to today's world, and the conflicts inherent in the human psyche.

Exercise of presence in your here/now: Five senses

This exercise helps you return to the here and now through sensory awareness. You can do it at any time of day.

1. Stop for a moment

Take a deep breath. Inhale through your nose for a count of four seconds. For four seconds, exhale through your mouth to the count of four. Do this two or three times.

2. Observe your environment and mentally answer:

Five things you notice: Look around you and name five things you notice out loud. It can be any detail: a plant, a shadow, a texture.

Four things you can touch: feel the texture of your clothes, the floor beneath your feet, the chair you're sitting in.

Three things you can hear: pay attention to the sounds: a voice, the hum of an appliance, the wind.

Two things you can smell: The scent in the air, on your clothes, on your skin, or simply notice the absence of odor.

Something you can taste: You can pay attention to the flavor in your mouth, or drink some water and notice its freshness.

3. Praise at least one of those sensations:

It doesn't matter which one. The mere fact of being able to perceive it, makes it already present. There are people in the world who can't smell, or touch, or see.

THANK YOURSELF: Thanking yourself for being mindful and present today is a profound act of self-love. Here are some ways to do it:

Recognizing yourself with loving words. Say something like:

"Thank you (your name) for being here, for choosing this body and this life, these people and this work, for not abandoning me in the noise of the world."

"Thank you for being there, even when it's hard."

"I'm proud of having chosen me at this moment."

Say these loving words out loud in front of the mirror or silently with your hand on your heart to enhance the effect, giving you a gesture of affection.

You can give yourself a hug, a caress, close your eyes for a moment and smile gently. Your body also registers gratitude.

Write it to yourself. Grab a notebook and write:

"Today I was present when..."

"I am grateful for..."

"What I value about myself today is..."

Writing it down anchors the experience and transforms it into an emotional memory.

Celebrate yourself with a small ritual: Make yourself a cup of tea, a glass of wine, play some soft music, light a candle, watch a soccer game with the kids – whatever feels right for you. Let that moment be a gift to yourself.

Simply breathe and smile. Sometimes a deep sigh and a conscious smile are already an act of internal gratitude. There's nothing else to do. Just be.

ASK: What was the climax moment where you said, "Enough is enough. This isn't working for me (job, relationship, place, etc.)?" Is it worth having it all if you don't truly have freedom? What do you want to choose today that will create your tomorrow?

ANSWER:_____

_____

_____

_____

_____

KEY TRUTH: The here and now is the only place where we truly exist. Often, we get lost in the past or the future; the rational mind, the conditioned mind, takes us there. The key is to recognize that the present is the only possible space for creation and transformation. We cannot change the past. We cannot intervene in the future. Your here and now, your present, is the only thing that can be changed. And that's why it has that name, because it truly is a gift.

THE QUALITY OF YOUR CONNECTIONS WITH THE OUTSIDE WORLD REFLECTS THE QUALITY OF THE CONNECTION YOU HAVE WITH YOURSELF, WITHIN.

When we learn to inhabit ourselves in the now without judgment, without excessive expectations or the pressure of time, we find a clarity that allows us to choose with awareness and freedom.

Only in this moment is there the opportunity to let go of what weighs us down, to appreciate what already is, and to build what we desire. If you could fully focus on this moment, what would you choose to feel or create right now?

Chapter 8: Resilience

THE SILENCE BROKEN. REPORT OF ABUSE

From survival to the reconstruction of identity

From that first 7-year-old patient to the present, I have treated in my office people who have experienced the trauma of sexual abuse in childhood or at some point during their adolescence.

Since my teaching position with Bettina Calvi, a professor specializing in this subject, during my time at the Faculty of Psychology in Rosario, Argentina, I have been deeply impacted by these stories. Violated bodies, shocked psyches, depression, aggression toward one's own body, a life that mutates into a kind of eternal pause; a person unable to stop hurting.

Having suffered sexual abuse is a deeply traumatic event. And if that abuse comes from the person who was supposed to protect you in your childhood, your father or mother, that abuse further transforms into the most horrific sinister act the psyche can endure: incest.

As a therapist, it hasn't been easy for me to sustain these healing processes. And many times I felt like I couldn't. What could I say to a patient whose innocence, joy of life, and childhood were robbed of them in the most insane way?

But just as actions can be pure horror, words can be a balm that heals with patience, respect, and love.

Child sexual abuse leaves profound psychological scars, affecting not only a person's daily life but also their intimacy, self-esteem, self-love, and ability to trust others.

However, healing is possible and can lead to a complete transformation of the being.

The Broken Silence: *Patients' truths*

"He would come into my room, lie down on my bed, and whisper in my ear that I shouldn't say anything, that it was a game between us, and that we couldn't tell Mommy."

For years, I lived in silence, trapped in a prison of guilt, shame, and fear. The abuse I suffered in my childhood robbed me of everything: my innocence, my parents' love, my own love, my trust in any adult who was around, and the ability to see myself as a whole being. I became a kind of soulless body, almost a robot that functions but isn't there. It took many years of searching for strategies to hide myself, of denying the pain my body felt, of not wanting anyone to get close, not even friends, much less a partner. I feel like the abuse put my life on hold, freezing it in a timeless time. I no longer know who I am or should be. I also don't feel like I can love anyone.

How do you live again when you feel like you're dead inside?

I don't know how to do it, I don't know if I have the strength to face that pain again.

One morning, after almost six months of attending sessions every week, I woke up and decided to break the silence. Speaking was the first step toward my freedom. The path to the beginning of my own healing process. I thought I didn't want to be a victim anymore. That I needed to regain control of my life. It wasn't linear, nor liberating from the start. Rather, I felt like I was returning to those years of horror. But you held not only your gaze, the anguish, and the tears, but my entire body with your presence. And that did help lift a huge burden off my shoulders. You made me see that I wasn't guilty of that violence. That I was a child. That I couldn't defend myself. And that others had to take care of me. You made me see myself again without disgust, without pain, without shame, without guilt. You managed to get those words out of my body and stop cutting, burning, and hating myself. With your patience and gentleness, you made me...come back to trust someone... I know it's a process with ups and downs. And that I have to keep walking. But with your help and the group support therapy, I'm beginning to rebuild my identity. I'm learning to recognize that abuse doesn't define who I am. And although each session is a battle won against the pain, my self-esteem grows stronger every day. I'm rebuilding myself and loving myself a little more. For me, regaining my self-esteem was fundamental. Because I literally wanted to die. I confronted the negative beliefs that abuse had implanted in my mind, my body, and my entire person. You showed me another perspective on abuse. I'm a survivor, and I have a lot to share. I'm beginning to recognize my achievements; and I'm seeing myself with compassion and respect. And although I'm not interested in forgiving my abuser, at least for now, I believe that in time I'll be able to let go of this limitation as well.

I am aware that forgiving does not mean forgetting or justifying the damage, but free myself from weight of hatred and resentment. We've talked about it a thousand times. I still can't! I'm learning to be patient with myself. You made me appreciate that being patient with my processes is okay. Forgiving my aggressor is an act of self-love that will take me more time.

Today, after almost 2 years of therapy, I consider myself a survivor, not a victim. I have changed my pain to purpose. I am helping others who have been through similar experiences. And it has empowered me to live with greater security and joy in my life.

Forgiveness in the context of child sexual abuse is a deeply emotional process, personal and complex. It is not about justifying or minimizing the damage suffered, but of a conscious decision that can contribute to the emotional healing of the victim. According to psychology, this process involves an internal change in the victim who can reduce emotional distress and avoidance behaviors or revenge.

It is essential to recognize that forgiveness is not mandatory or essential for all victims. Each person must evaluate whether this path is appropriate for their process of psychic repair. A forgiveness misunderstanding or imposed in a therapeutic space, can weaken a person's ability to protect themselves, making them more vulnerable and facilitating the continuation of the abuse.

Forgiveness, when freely chosen, can be a powerful tool to free the person from the weight of resentment and allow him or her to move toward a fuller life. However, it is essential that this process be approached with sensitivity and respect for each individual's time and needs.

Ultimately, it's an option that must be carefully considered, always prioritizing the patient's mental health and autonomy. It's an act of self-love that, if chosen, can significantly contribute to personal growth.

Forgiveness doesn't mean forgetting or minimizing what happened. It means freeing ourselves from the weight of resentment that binds us to the past and prevents us from moving forward. It means healing our wounds and regaining inner peace.

This act is a gift we give ourselves. It's an affirmation that we deserve to live without the chains of hatred and bitterness. We don't change the past, but we transform our present and open the door to a freer, more conscious, present, and fulfilling future.

Forgiveness is a process, sometimes long and painful, but deeply liberating. It is a path that allows us to recover our power and our dignity.

I want to close this chapter by encouraging all those who have gone through a similar experience to seek support and remind them that they are not alone.

While childhood sexual abuse leaves lifelong scars, overcoming it can be the beginning of a path toward resilience and transformation. Each story of survival is a testament to strength and courage.

If you are reading this and have had such an experience, remember that your voice matters, that your pain matters, that you deserve to be heard, and that help is available. Healing is possible, and every step toward that state is an act of self-love and justice for your being.

YOU ARE NOT ALONE!

And although hopelessness, sadness, and overwhelmment may be your daily life today, you have known that your story can be the inspiration others need to uncover theirs and heal as well.

I am aware that your scars are not only the visible ones, but that you have others that are deeper and more painful, defying any human capacity for reconstruction.

Yet you're here, reading this, and that means your story is one of survival, a testament to your inherent strength. You're reading this; you survived a terribly traumatic experience, and you're moving forward. Your pain doesn't define who you are, but your courage to face it does.

Returning to yourself isn't a linear, challenge-free path. It's a process that will require time, patience, and, above all, support. I want you to know that there are people, communities, and resources willing to walk with you, to listen, and to support you in your darkest moments.

Remember that "speaking is an act of liberation," and "seeking help is an act of courage." I kept moving forward, I know that you can do it. Your story matters to me, your voice matters to me, and your life is priceless. Even though it may seem difficult today, the light that you require is within you. And so is the strength.

Allow yourself to return to yourself, to smile again, because you deserve to live the life you want.

I'm aware that the abuse left its mark on your body, your mind, and your soul. It's not just an emotional wound, but an experience that disconnected you from everything and everyone, from your essence and your own capacity to feel.

Don't permit it to return and take refuge in your body. Breathe consciously, you are still alive. Every movement, every gesture of self-care is an act of repair – a step toward putting together the broken pieces – and returning to your freedom.

Embracing your pain does not entail justifying it or perpetuating it, but rather acknowledging it, giving it space, and allowing yourself to navigate it with compassion. It's understanding that this pain is part of your history, but it doesn't have to define your future. Dare to reconnect with your emotions, permit yourself to feel guilt-free again, and regain confidence in your own body as a place of life, not violence.

BE KIND TO IT!

If you are reading this and felt that the road is uphill, remember that within you there is an immense force that still beats. It has not been extinguished. That every tear is a manifestation of love for yourself. And every cry, an act of resistance and rebirth.

YOU ARE NOT ALONE!

There are many beings here willing to accompany you. And in your life there is still room for joy, fulfillment, and love.

Feeling alive again is possible, and it begins the moment we dare to embrace ourselves completely, with all our scars and all our light.

You survived. I admire your courage. I respect your integrity, and impulse to continue loving yourself every day.

FORGIVENESS ISN'T AN ACT DIRECTED AT YOUR ABUSER.

IT'S AN ACT OF PROFOUND SELF-LOVE.

YOU'RE CHOOSING YOURSELF OVER ANY ACT OF VIOLENCE THAT A

"PSYCHOPATH" INFLICTED ON YOU.

YOU'RE CHOOSING YOUR WELL-BEING OVER YOUR PAIN.

YOU'RE AFFIRMING THAT YOU CHOSE TO LIVE WITH PEACE AND HOPE.

YOU ARE CHOOSING YOURSELF ABOVE ANY HARM.

FORGIVING THOSE WHO HAVE HURT US DEEPLY IS A DECLARATION

THAT MEANS YOU — YOUR WELL-BEING — IS MORE IMPORTANT

THAN THE PAIN. DON'T FORGET THAT.

Writing about this topic is truly delicate. It requires sensitivity from both the reader and the writer. An approach that shows respect for those who suffered; and at the same time empathy, hope, and strength.

It hasn't been easy for me to develop, but I consider it deeply necessary, for those who were able to speak and for all those who remain silent.

Every patient who confided their journey to me has my eternal love. This chapter is a tribute to the immense courage of each and every one of them.

Chapter 9: Healing

Words are not carried away by the wind,
they are carried away by the body.
Notice that it's a choice and it's your responsibility.

THE BODY NEVER BETRAYS US ... IT ADAPTS

The body can generate excess weight as protection. If we suffer abandonment, the lungs can close up due to sadness. If we carry the guilt that was passed on to us, the pancreas can become upset. If we are forced to swallow situations, the stomach suffers. We grow feeling that our material support is going to be missing, the heart resents it.

Nothing is accidental. Every physical illness is first fueled by unmanaged emotions, by internal conflicts experienced in solitude and silence because the unconscious doesn't distinguish between the real, the imaginary, or the symbolic – it simply obeys.

When an emotional shock sets in, the brain sends a precise order to an organ – the spinal cord – to help us survive, sending nerve impulses and commands to different parts of the body because its sole function is to keep us alive.

We don't die just because of a diagnosis. We die slowly every time we silence what hurts, every time our being cries out for help and we ignore it.

Illness is the last language our self uses to awaken us. It's the cry we get when we don't listen to our intuition, when we block out tears, when we swallow anger, when we numb fear, or deny our history.

THE BODY SPEAKS. AND IF WE DON'T LISTEN... IT SCREAMS

When we become aware of this, we begin to help ourselves. Nothing out there is going to cure you, if you don't begin to recognize everything that was stuck in your body due to a lack of words and choosing to heal it within yourself.

Let's face it, medicine doesn't cure, it patches. It supports a system designed for disease.

What would happen if we were all healthy? Would doctors, hospitals, the pharmaceutical industry, health insurance, and all the associated businesses still exist? Of course not.

Since modern medicine began to organize, back in the 5th century BC with Hippocrates, we've assumed that health is something external. Science advanced, but it focused on artificially prolonging life. More prosthetics, more antibiotics, more vaccines, more interventions.

However, my beautiful reader, healing isn't a destination, it's a journey. And it begins the day you ask yourself: *What wounds am I ready to release now?*

People don't die from illnesses, they die from emotions they were never able to recognize and manage.

But how do we heal?

Well, we begin to heal when we stop looking solely at the symptom and begin to recognize, to look directly at, to see the history that inscribes it in our body. We heal when we abandon the fantasy that something external will fix what we didn't want to face at the time. We heal when we dare to descend into the dizzying basement of the emotional world, where the trauma, loss, humiliation, abandonment, or violence occurred.

The body doesn't need to be healed. It needs to be listened to – understood – embraced – loved.

The disease is not a punishment. It's a call from your being to return to yourself. Listen to it. Thank yourself. And then, let go.

Because when you heal your emotions, you heal your body. What you don't express, your body will manifest – whether you believe it or not – whether you understand it or not – whether you accept it or deny it.

Whatever you heal in your being, your body celebrates with health and vitality. We are not just flesh, as traditional medicine encourages us to maintain. We are history, emotions, vibration, and soul.

Healing is a journey. It begins when you stop fearing the truth you carry within you.

I already explained in another chapter how neuropsychology – which studies the relationship between the nervous system and psychological processes – together with biopsychology and epigenetics, show the causal relationships that exist between the environment, human behavior, and the latter's ability to extend or shorten our own lives.

For years, I've been fascinated by studying the relationship between emotions, biological processes, how we perceive reality, and our environment. And in these 20 years of caring for patients, I've found that the flexible and dynamic interplay of these layers is what keeps people in optimal health, regardless of their chronological age.

Unmanaged traumatic emotional experiences largely influence the processes of disease and cellular deterioration that lead to death. Thus, by recalling the origin of our internal conflicts, we can consciously unblock them and release the emotions that remain stuck in the body, which years later generate physical illness.

Although this is not the only way to achieve this, it is also known that if we provide ourselves with a richer natural environment, for example, the intensity of these emotions can diminish and they can be expressed more gently without negatively impacting our body.

Fundamental requirements for human health is consciousness, nutrition and movement.

We've sat still since the dawn of civilization, and we haven't moved. So much so that we had to develop an artificial space to generate what our ancestors did while moving around the land. We call them gyms.

Being able to think and understand the interaction of mind, emotions, body, and environment in a circular and collaborative way, is what will give you a life rich in joy and health. This is not just a physical thing, but also a psycho-emotional, mental, environmental and cultural inter-action.

Thus, by changing our perceptions, our perspectives change. And by changing how we interpret the events of our lives, we can dynamically transform our entire reality and dramatically improve our health, fitness, and prosperity.

Our family history, beliefs, and past experiences greatly influence how we react to life. From a young age, we absorb patterns, values, and perspectives that shape how we interpret the world and how we face challenges.

If we grew up in an environment where security and emotional support were constant, we are likely to develop confidence and resilience. Conversely, if our environment was marked by criticism, abandonment, or lack of affection, we may react with fear, mistrust, or extreme self-demand in adulthood.

Inherited beliefs also influence our decisions. We often act on commands we don't even question:

• You have to work twice as hard to be successful.

• Love always hurts

• Health depends only on genetics

• Eat everything on your plate because there are people who are starving.

We end up eating out of guilt, growing up with injected fears and exhausting our bodies because "without sacrifice it seems like there's no value. "

When we allow ourselves to reexamine these fixed, and very limiting, ideas or points of view, we can finally begin to break cycles of pain and build a vision more aligned with our true essence.

Our social environment reinforces or challenges what we carry with us from our history. Therefore, surrounding ourselves with people who have a different perspective on life, who encourage us to grow, help us question what limits us, and accompany us in our transformation process are key to expanding our overall well-being.

We heal ourselves when we stop seeing illness or symptoms as an enemy and begin to understand them as a message from our body, a reflection of our emotions and our history. Health isn't something external; it doesn't depend solely on a pill or a medical procedure. It's a profound process that integrates the mind, body, emotions, and environment.

Some suggestions:

• Listen to your body: It speaks to us constantly, but we often ignore its signals. Recurring ailments, fatigue, muscle tension, digestive problems, dermatitis – all have a source beyond the physical. By consciously observing these symptoms, we can recognize the message they bring us.

•Learn to manage unresolved emotions: Repressed emotions can manifest as illness. Anger, sadness, fear – everything finds its way out. Allowing yourself to feel, express, and release these emotions is essential for self-healing.

• Change your perception of illness: Instead of seeing it as a punishment or a bodily failure, value it as an adaptation, a biological response to an internal conflict. Changing the way you interpret your health transforms your reality.

• Connect with your own story: Many of our ailments are related to past experiences, childhood wounds, and inherited beliefs. We heal when we dare to look there without fear and free ourselves from the burdens that no longer belong to us.

• Change your habits and environment: What we eat, how we sleep, the level of stress we handle, the quality of our relationships, and exposure to toxic emotions – everything influences our health. Making small, everyday changes has a profound impact on self-healing.

• Raise your energetic vibration: Healing, or being healthy, isn't just physical. It's also energetic. Changing your cellular wave frequency, getting your vibrations to fall within certain levels – through thoughts, emotions, words, actions – modifies how cells respond. Practicing gratitude, generating joy, and freeing yourself from the past allows biology to transform. Create kind and prosperous environments. What you see every day also influences your health.

Healing isn't about eliminating a symptom, but rather discovering the message behind it, understanding it, and allowing the body to return to its natural balance. There is no external medicine more powerful than the ability to return to yourself with awareness and love.

Which part of this process resonates most with you? Which one are you currently on?

COMPREHENSIVE WELLNESS EXERCISE: THE PILLARS OF HEALTH

This exercise is practical and easy to implement into your daily routine. Its goal is to help you maintain physical, mental, and emotional balance.

1. Daily Movement (Exercise - 5 minutes minimum) It doesn't have to be strenuous, just consistent. Simple options:

- Walk a few minutes outdoors.
- Stretching when you wake up or before going to sleep.
- Dance to a lively song.
- Use stairs instead of the elevator.

2. Conscious Nutrition (Eating, Healthy Choices) It's not about diets, but about smart choices. Before each meal, ask yourself, "Does this food give me energy or take it away?" Prioritize less processed foods, more nutrients, and good hydration.

3. Restful sleep (Sleep - 10 minutes of disconnection before continuing/ 8 hours at night) Quality rest impacts physical and mental health.

- Avoid screens 10 minutes before bedtime.
- Breathe deeply and relax your body.
- Create a small nighttime ritual (reading, quiet music, writing).

• Maintain stable sleep schedules.

4. Connection with the environment (Environment - 3 minutes of contact with nature) Our well-being is regulated by being in contact with the earth, the air and the sun.

> • Touch a plant; pet a pet.
>
> • Look at the sky and breathe fresh air.
>
> • Walking barefoot on grass or sand.

5. Emotional Management (Self-observation - 2 minutes a day to check your well-being) At the end of the day, ask yourself:"How did I feel today?" "What did I do right for my health?" "What can I improve tomorrow?" This moment of review allows you to adjust habits and strengthen your emotional well-being.

THANK YOURSELF: I thank myself for beginning to see what I didn't want to see. I thank myself for listening to my body instead of silencing it. I thank myself for having become aware that every symptom, every pain, every tension, is not an enemy, but a message. A reflection of what I kept quiet, of what I didn't confront, of what my soul needed to express.

I thank myself for recognizing that my biology isn't wrong, that my body is only seeking to adapt, to protect me, to show me what I didn't want to hear. I thank myself for stopping and observing. For choosing not to ignore what makes me uncomfortable. For encouraging me to decipher the internal codes that once seemed like a condemnation and that today I understand as calls to awaken.

I thank myself for allowing myself to change. For letting go of the idea that healing means correcting, when in reality it means integrating, accepting, embracing. I thank myself for learning that medicine is not the only answer and that my well-being does not depend exclusively on external factors. For understanding that true healing begins within me, in every choice, in every thought, in every emotion that I experience and let them flow instead of repressing them.

I thank myself for trusting my intuition, for listening to the signs, for transforming pain into understanding. I thank myself for not being a victim of my illness, but the protagonist of my well-being. For recognizing that no one can save me but myself.

I thank myself for daring to question. For stopping expecting quick fixes and starting to observe the story behind each symptom. I thank myself for being aware that healing is not a destination, but a path.

I thank myself because today I choose to listen to myself. And in doing so, I begin to heal.

ASK: When I think I have all the answers, it's time to ask new questions. What if you asked new questions? What if you chose the possibility your illness is showing you, instead of the limitation?

We all have the infinite power to transform our lives, and yet 99 percent of the inhabitants of this planet choose powerlessness as their favorite incarnation.

What are you going to start choosing? Miracles do exist, but you have to work for them. Sometimes we don't even realize it, and we're so angry; you're not being yourself. When you're too sad, you're not being yourself. How many of you are constantly trying to be at peace or avoiding conflict?

All of these are implants, and they don't allow us to expand. All of these considerations and all of that energetic burden are what's causing us to feel uneasy and getting sick.

ANSWER: _____

_____

_____

_____

_____

_____

KEY TRUTH: Being healthy isn't a destination; it's a journey, and it's a choice. The body doesn't betray us; it reveals to us what we haven't yet heard. When we stop fighting the symptom and begin to understand the history that shapes it within us, true transformation begins.

Chapter 10: Invest in You

Invest in Women is to transform the world

Let us increasingly be transformative women

THE ENTREPRENEURIAL FORCE

What are you going to do this year for the first time?

Every new cycle brings unique opportunities. The question isn't just what you're going to do, but why do you want to do it. Because when a dream begins to take shape, true entrepreneurial power is activated.

Who are you and what did you want to be, as a girl, when you grew up?

The initial desire, the one that moved us in childhood, is no coincidence. Often, the entrepreneurial journey is a return to those forgotten dreams, to that genuine force that was pulsing within us from the very beginning.

Where there's a will, there's a way... or is there just a will to keep trying?

Sometimes, power isn't in the immediate result, but in the consistency of action. Because it's not just about achieving it, it's about continuing to believe in what we do, even when the path is challenging.

FEMALE ENTREPRENEURSHIP IN FIGURES

In Argentina, almost 60 percent of female entrepreneurs are between 30 and 50 years old, and only 8 percent are between 18 and 30. The most popular areas are retail, gastronomy, and apparel, often driven by the need for financial independence, the enormous wage gap, and the lack of opportunities in the traditional labor market.

The reality is clear: the trend is not helping. If you're a woman, you're an entrepreneur. If you're a man, you're a businessman.

The decision to start a business. A one-way street?

Entrepreneurship means taking risks and challenging established norms. It means changing structures and breaking down imposed boundaries. As women, we often face a market that isn't designed for us, and that's why the processes of expansion and growth can be more complex. However, this difficulty also drives us to be transformative.

The emotional and financial costs of entrepreneurship will be there. You have to learn not to blame yourself for them.

Entrepreneurship confronts us with various internal dilemmas:

- Why do I have a hard time talking about money? With whom do I have a hard time talking about money? Why? Who am I giving my numbers to?

- What things have I been saying yes to, when I want to shout no?

- What cost do I pay to sustain what does not add up for me?

- Why do I think delegating will cost me my presence in the business?

- How ambitious are you? And if so, is it wrong?

Learning to speak honestly about all these issues without blame is key to the entrepreneurial journey. **Being generous, yes. Working for free, no.**

Isn't entrepreneurship just about having a business?

Women are born entrepreneurs not only out of necessity, but because we live in a world that constantly challenges us. Entrepreneurship isn't just about starting a business; it's a way of looking at the world, of transforming what surrounds us.

The key is sustainability. Your business shouldn't tie you down 24/7. Growth comes when the business is part of your life, but not the entirety of it.

The potential of your business: You'll recognize it when you can share what caused you to fall in life and how your business lifted you up. Success stories are filled with previous failures. We are not what happens to us; we are what we do with what happens to us.

HEROINES IN A WORLD DESIGNED EXCLUSIVELY FOR HEROES

Female leadership has always been secondary in history, because the world was designed for women to be the protagonists. But we are transformative women, not transformed women.

We didn't come to adapt, but to change the rules of the game – to challenge the norms and build our own narrative.

Your greatest value: daring to flourish

Every woman has a unique story. Each has intrinsic value that is destined to flourish.

If you have a burning desire, do it. Yes, it will have a cost. That's why, on the path of entrepreneurship, it is essential to have allies, women who hold, accompaniment and impulse.

Being an entrepreneur is a constant learning process of trusting yourself and recognizing that you can always shine. The only real competition is with yourself.

Developing the network as a transformative force. We use a very small percentage of our human potential. When we connect online, everything expands. Alone, we can go fast. Networked, we go far.

HOW I REACHED MY PERSONAL BEST

My journey has been a circular movement, where various areas of health converge to enhance each person's holistic development. My goal is and has always been to empower you to be who you truly are and recognize your own knowledge, leaving behind external elements that no longer identify you.

Through my experience, I seek to support others at different stages of their journey so they can redefine their own experiences.

My Career

I am Veronica Alonso, a psychologist, psychoanalyst, and wellness coach. I turned my name and profession into a personal brand, integrating innovative tools, learning new techniques, and specializing in various areas of mental health and wellness. This is how I developed a clinical practice that not only helps release trauma but also dynamically improves the lives of every patient who enters my office.

My mentoring program provides tools to enhance personal, professional, and career development. Through it, I help to build a road map to detox, in which they learn to identify skills or potential, overcome fears and limiting beliefs, manage material resources, strengthen their presence in the world without being defined by anything, and, above all, to incorporate enjoyment and ease into every aspect of life.

Despite having more than 20 years of professional experience, I always considered myself an entrepreneur. I made my way into the healthcare field without having any family members in the field to anchor me initially and without seeking more traditional structures, such as an employment relationship. I am a freelancer.

My Professional Experience

Throughout my career, I have worked in various areas:

- Businesswoman, with experience in:
- Human Resources of Sipar Aceros.
- Motivation and coaching of athletes.
- Accompanying people with terminal illnesses.
- Care for children in situations of social risk.
- Clinic for anxiety disorders, grief, depression, and phobias.

My specialization in child psychology changed when my daughter was born. I decided to focus on working with adults to preserve my energy and provide the best care to each patient and my growing little one.

I currently reside in Florida, United States. For the past 5 years, I have been generating digital content and virtually serving patients from Argentina, Chile, Peru, Colombia, Mexico, and Spain.

I am the Director of Rehabilitation and Work Accessibility at Growing for Inclusion, a foundation dedicated to the inclusion of people with disabilities (PWD) and adapted sports as a tool for social integration.

My Expansion and Studies

The last few years have been key in my professional evolution:

I focused on neuroplasticity. I studied the most cutting-edge techniques and practices of personal development and energetic movement, working with specialists from around the world.

In Spain (2023) and in Italy (2024), I participated in conferences on the environment, epigenetics and their impact on health, longevity and motivation.

You Had to Be a Woman: My Philosophy

My brand is more than a title: it's a metaphor for life. It doesn't matter if you're a man or a woman; the name represents the stereotypes that limit us, oppress us, and prevent us from expanding our creative life force. True transformation comes when we manage to dismantle those stigmas and act autonomously, from our true desire.

This program is an interactive, circular space where we support each person's growth through tools from pragmatic psychology, wellness coaching, and depth psychology.

Why am I telling you this?

Because it's possible. Year after year, I paved my way, trusting my intuition, letting my perceptions guide me, acquiring new tools, adding them together I've leveraged my previous knowledge and adjusted my approach to grow holistically. Today, I'm the result of my own redesign. I went from being a passionate young woman to a self-managed, committed professional, and finally, a businesswoman or personal brand. I created a way of developing my work that dynamically improves the lives of the people who call me. I've generated many insights in them, living a more enjoyable life, and enjoying biodiversity.

Gratitude for those who trusted me and transformed themselves is what drives me to share everything I've learned. My mission is to offer you conscious support and real strategies for your evolution.

The Essence of Success

Well-being and success are not just external goals, but internal energies that we cultivate every day:

- Self-confidence, despite those who doubt us.
- Happiness, as daily vital energy.
- Kindness, in every internal process.
- Conscious nutrition, that nourishes the soul and not just calms hunger.
- Motion, because the body needs to be activated.
- Generative links, those that really add to our lives.
- Deep rest, that regenerate our cells.

My favorite phrase is:

A PERSON WHO INSPIRES OTHERS TO SHINE NOT ONLY LOVES THEMSELVES DEEPLY AND WELL, BUT ALSO KNOWS THERE'S ROOM FOR EVERYONE.

Exercise to start designing your business project today: Creating a Business Foundation

This exercise will help you define the vision, purpose, and first steps of your business. You can do it in a notebook or digital document.

1. Define Your Central Idea

Answer these questions honestly:

- What product or service do I want to offer?
- What problem does my business solve or what need does it meet?

• Who would be my ideal clients?

2. Analyze Your Differential

> • What makes my proposal unique?

> • How does it differ from what already exists on the market?

> • What values and principles do I want my business to represent?

3. Make a Resource Map

Identify what you have available and what you need: Personal resources (skills, knowledge, experience). Material resources (workspace, technology, tools). Financial resources (start-up capital, financing options).

4. Write Your Mission and Vision

The mission is what you do and why you do it. The vision is where you want to take your business in the future. Example: My mission is to empower women entrepreneurs with psychological and wellness tools to boost their businesses. My vision is to create an international community that fosters personal and professional growth.

5. Define Your First 3 Action Steps

Choose three concrete actions you can take TODAY to move forward: Research the market and competitors. Establish a network of strategic contacts. Create a list of potential clients and allies.

6. Growth Mindset

Think about the fears or limiting beliefs that might be holding you back from your venture. Write down:

> • What negative thoughts have stopped my progress?

> • How can I restructure them in empowering affirmations?

7. Create Your Elevator Pitch

An elevator pitch is a brief and powerful presentation of your business in less than a minute. State your idea clearly and enthusiastically, including: Who are you? What do you do? Why is it valuable?

Example: "I'm Veronica Alonso, a psychologist and wellness coach.

I help entrepreneurs enhance their well-being and leadership through comprehensive strategies. My goal is for each person to transform their potential into real success."

THANK YOURSELF: Before finishing, write a statement about your business: "I trust in my vision, my skills, and my ability to create the business I want." Remember that this is just the first step, but the most important thing is to get started. Are you ready to take the first step on your project today?

ASK: Do you feel small? When you feel this way, nothing big can be revealed in your reality. What if you gave yourself permission to expand, to go beyond your body, your mental limitations, your family upbringing, your city? What if you simply allowed yourself to recognize that as a body you have limits, but as the being that inhabits it, you don't? This isn't visualization; this is activating your own energy. This will help you get moving.

ANSWER:_____

_____

_____

_____

_____

KEY TRUTH: Entrepreneurship is more than starting a business; it's a way of life based on autonomy, creativity, and resilience.

Some things you need to know:

• Fear is part of the process, but NOT a hindrance. Uncertainty will always be present; the important thing is to make decisions with confidence and learn from mistakes.

• There's no perfect time to start. START NOW. If you wait until you have everything figured out, you'll never take the first step. The ideal is to start with what you have and adjust along the way.

• Your personal brand is your differentiator. Beyond what you sell, people connect with your story, your authenticity, and the transformation you can offer.

• Failure isn't the end; it's part of the growth process. Every set-back gives you valuable information about what to improve, adjust, or re-think.

• Networks and alliances BOOST your business. No one grows alone. Connecting with other entrepreneurs, sharing knowledge, and collaborating opens up new opportunities.

• Money is important, but passion is the driving force. Starting a business with purpose is what will allow you to sustain your business for the long term, even in difficult times.

• Discipline is more powerful than motivation. You'll have days when you don't feel like moving forward, but consistency and commitment make the difference.

If you're about to start your project, I recommend writing your own key truth about entrepreneurship. What learning do you want to implement today to build your path? What do you want to see manifested in the world? Dream in a big way, there is time to shrink.

Chapter 11: Demand the Universe

How are you choosing to live your life?

Ask and it shall be given to you. Consciousness does not judge; it is absolute permission.

Being fortunate doesn't necessarily have to do with something random like luck, but rather with the choices we make daily and throughout our lives.

We've been taught from a young age that elections, at least for the generation between 30 and 50, are once and for all. We've grown up with that demand and fear of making mistakes because if they're once and for all, they better be the best ones for us.

In truth, this isn't the case. We should constantly be involved in choosing every single thing that has to do with our lives. And forever is a myth. Choices are for as long as they last. That is, as long as they make us happy, as long as they generate joy, and as long as they allow us greater abundance or prosperity.

There's a universal law that states: to receive, we must be willing to give. It's a kind of symbolic exchange without explicitness. And it makes sense, because if you only give and there's never anything in return, an imbalance occurs that ends up depleting whatever you want to build. Now, giving should never mean suffering. If it hurts, then it's not there. If you constantly feel an immense emptiness in your chest, that place isn't nourishing you.

Another universal law is the fundamental principle that everything in the universe vibrates. This is known as the law of resonance.

And…how do we use the law of resonance to create the life we want?

Our thoughts, emotions, words, and actions emit energetic frequencies. And these frequencies aren't lost in the void: they resonate and attract similar vibrations.

To put it simply, anything that vibrates at a certain wavelength attracts experiences, people, and circumstances that vibrate compatibly at that same frequency.

We don't necessarily attract what we mentally desire, but rather what we are emotionally vibrating in the depths of our being. What resonates energetically in every microparticle of our body.

If your vibration today is tinged with fear, scarcity, or anger, for example, you will unconsciously attract more situations that make you feel that way.

If, on the other hand, your vibration is one of gratitude, trust, love, or joy, you will attract more of that into your life.

Resonance is like an internal music that only the right ears can hear.

Your life thus becomes an echo of your inner state. A symphony of possibilities that will attract certain notes, creating a score that will in turn be perfectly compatible with the symphony it will attract.

This law also teaches us that it's not about "forcing" changes from the outside, but rather about working on our internal vibration – our own melody.

When you genuinely change what you feel and think, the external world inevitably begins to change.

In short, everything in the universe was created with an energetic balance. You can't just give and not receive. You don't attract your opposite, but what's similar. It's not about manifesting, it's about being. We are a vibrational magnet. Your current emotional state is the signal you're sending to the universe. And the universe, like a mirror, returns to you a reality that resonates with all these chords.

Our thoughts, feelings, emotions, and actions create our reality. By consistently focusing our attention on who we are – rather than what we fear – we can attract the experiences we desire into our present.

You are a creator. You are constantly shaping your reality through your thoughts, beliefs, and emotions, consciously or unconsciously.

These laws are always active. You attract what is inside of you.

Your emotional state is your compass: if you felt well, you're in tune with your natural inner self. If you feel bad, you've disconnected from that coherence that aligns thought, emotion, feeling, and action.

Consciousness is a state of you as an infinite being in which permission consists of not only asking, but also allowing yourself to receive – all without judging anything. That happens when you maintain your state of well-being, without resistances such as fear, doubt, worry or control.

Everything you desire already exists in a "vibrational now": as soon as you imagine it, it has already been energetically created. Your responsibility is to align yourself vibrationally to experience it in your physical reality.

When you assume, you create expectations or projections about how something should be. If it doesn't happen the way you wanted, then, instead of feeling frustration, you learn to choose more fun.

Because consciousness, dear reader, isn't a serious thing. It's a grand invitation to be more of yourself, even in your less elegant expressions. We grow and become stronger when we stop seeking external validation.

What's valuable is already within you, within who you are. You don't need to prove anything to anyone. Your light, your worth, your essence can be perceived from afar. And those who didn't notice your presence, believe me: they will notice your absence.

The truest love, the deepest and most necessary love is the one you should have for yourself.

So, work on your inner self, beat your ego, walk your own path, and emerge from this transformation more yourself than ever. Everyone must do their part. And when the time is right, the right people will be attracted to you naturally, effortlessly, and with synergy.

It's not just about loving others. It's about loving yourself first and foremost. From there you can build connections, spaces, and a more genuine world.

Don't settle for less than you deserve. It is not always comfortable, easy or pleasant to be the light for so many. But if that's your gift, you can't turn it off. It was given to you to share, to touch hearts.

You have a gift: that of emotional healing. Be your own light, your own guide, your own hope. Everything has its reward.

And if someone comes into your life, hope they leave better than they came in. That's your mission, even if they don't always recognize it.

POWERED by that energy, of what you give, of what you sow – when you help others, your glow intensifies.

Finding the balance between shining a light on others and not dimming your own light sometimes means not just leaving, but changing how you stay.

Souls are chosen before this existence to share lessons. There are no mistakes in soul encounters, nor are there coincidences. Everything responds to an evolutionary plan of consciousness. It may be difficult for you to assimilate, but that is the most important truth to assimilate in this life.

Trust in the knowledge of your being and surrender to every other person who comes into your life. What you attract is exactly what you need. Explore it without fear.

There are magical places in the world where the connection to the Earth is felt with less interference than here. Places where we are nourished in so many ways – non-cognitive, but very obvious – that our consciousness cannot help but awaken.

I ask you to connect with this image, feel it throughout your entire body, and remember: *where did you feel this way? And with whom?*

Now look around you and be honest: every time you communicate something, is there a blockage on the other side? Then that space is too small for you.

You must learn to let go and fly.

INTEGRATION EXERCISE: RESCHEDULING MY ELECTION

1. Find a moment of silence where you can be alone with yourself, without interruptions.

2. Take a sheet of paper and divide it into two columns:

In the first column write: "Where I stay out of habit or (etc.)"

In the second column write: "Where I would really like to be."

3. Reflect with complete honesty:

In what areas, relationships, or situations are you "swimming against the current" today; feeling burdened, suffering, or disconnected?

What spaces, people, or activities make me feel expanded, light, and emotionally nourished?

4. Choose a small but concrete step to start getting closer to those places where you can fly.

Example: Deciding not to insist where there is a blockage, or starting to look for environments that nourish your vibration.

5. Affirmation to anchor:

Say it out loud (or write it down and read it)

Today I choose to open myself to receive all that nourishes me, and I let go of all that weighs me down. My light knows the way.

LIFE EXERCISE: THE MAP OF MY CHOICES

Every choice we make is a seed we plant in our lives. Some seeds grow and nourish us; others weigh like stones that hinder our progress.

I invite you to do this exercise calmly, feeling each word.

1. Find a quiet moment. Choose a comfortable place, perhaps with a lit candle or some object that connects you to your inner strength.

2. Close your eyes and connect with your body.

Ask yourself, where do I feel the weight today in my body?

Close your eyes, connect with that proprioception, and notice which part of your body responds. Perhaps your chest, your throat, your stomach.

3. Take a sheet of paper and draw two circles:

In the first circle, write inside: "Choices that weigh on me."

In the second circle: "Elections that expand me."

4. Write in each circle without censorship.

Anything you feel today represents a burden, emptiness, or unnecessary effort.

Everything you feel in your life represents love, expansion, lightness, joy.

5. Choose a **single choice** that weighs less (even if it is small) and commit yourself to **transform it into action.**

It could be taking a walk somewhere you really like, letting go of something you've been holding onto for a while, starting an awkward conversation, or saying no to something you've been putting off out of fear.

6. To close:

Close your eyes again and repeat this phrase to yourself:

Today I choose with love. My life is a reflection of my choices. I am free to let go of what holds me down and embrace what makes me soar.

ANSWER: _____

_____

_____

_____

_____

_____

KEY TRUTH: Life does not reward those who try the hardest, but those who allow themselves to receive the most.

Remember that true power is in openness, not control.

Twilight

If you have yourself, you have everything!

Throughout this journey of stories, reflections, and tools, we've walked together on paths that invite us to look inward. We've talked about the importance of being present in our lives, consciously choosing each second, inhabiting the now with authenticity, without masks or disguises.

In a world saturated with distractions, external demands, and emotional absences, pausing to reconnect with our true essence is not only an act of courage but also a profound manifestation of self-love.

I sincerely invite you to continue exploring your own truths. Don't be afraid of questions; don't just look for answers, permit uncertainty and being out of control. Let the natural movement of life surprise you. Honor your path, with its lights and shadows because every day that shelters your eyes and breathe is a new possibility to discover yourself, to expand, and rewrite you.

Life isn't a straight line with a defined destination; it's a journey filled with constant fluctuations, an ocean of learning and transformation. It's never a point of arrival; it's always a new beginning.

If anything shared managed to ignite a spark within you, inspire reflection, or spark a small movement, then this work has already made sense because the only constant in life is change. And when you open yourself to it – when you allow life to flow through you without resistance – you discover that your being, your knowing, your allowing, and your receiving are deeply intertwined. Recognizing this is also an act of creation and freedom.

There are no absolute truths. There are no user manuals for good living. Only unique paths, like your soul, interesting points of view, and infinite beings traversing a finite experience. And in that mystery lies the beauty of being alive.

Each person designs their reality based on the lens through which they choose to observe the world. I hope your lens is of gratitude, courage, compassion, and kindness. May it reflect the unique greatness of your journey through this life. And I also hope that your self-confidence will be your driving force and your intuition the compass that guides your journey.

Remember: every choice is as valid as the last. There are no mistakes, only experiences. There are no successes, only choices. Every step you take leaves traces, those of your essence. Because in the end, the journey, with all that it entails, is as sacred as the destination.

And this, perhaps, is just the beginning...

The time of constant demand deadlines. Productivity will no longer guide humanity. The entire planet has been pushing us to act, generate, and respond for decades. Standards of success have been, and still are, governed by aesthetic standards, by having or popularity, completely devoid of content.

Something else awaits us and our offspring.

I hope these chapters have allowed you to see this and that you are aware of your place and purpose in all of this. Your life is a gift; you were not born by mistake, you are not wrong, you are valuable. Permit yourself to discover the gift that you are and give it to the world.

In the midst of all this dehumanizing madness, it can be easy to lose sight of ourselves, to forget our essential truth. "You didn't come to have, you came to be." The other comes as a consequence of you being the creator of your own life project.

It becomes vital to wake up from the noise outside and inhabit our inner selves. And it is precisely in these moments of silence and reflection that we find the clarity to live with coherence, awareness, and constant choice.

This journey is not about achieving unattainable perfection, but rather about aligning each step with our deepest truth, with coherence in our existence.

Every choice we make, no matter how small, has the power to shape our experience. Being true to yourself is just as important as saying no in a timely manner, even when it's difficult or challenging. It's embracing our authenticity and allowing ourselves the vulnerability of embracing the gaps, recognizing that our choices have a significant impact on our lives and the lives of those around us.

There are no outsiders responsible. Your choice creates, even if your choice is silence, separation, or indifference.

Mindfulness, on the other hand, invites us to be present, to live each moment with mindfulness, and to make informed decisions. It allows us to identify our strengths and areas for improvement. It offers us this opportunity to constantly grow and evolve. When we are mindful, we stop acting on autopilot and begin to live intentionally, meaningfully.

Choosing reminds us that we always have the power to decide. We are not victims of our circumstances; we are the architects of our destiny. Every choice is an opportunity to align ourselves with our values and principles, and to build a life that reflects our true essence.

Move to the life that sincerely you want. Don't wait any longer. Stop hurting. Dare to feel and be.

Keep exploring your own truths, question everything and everyone. Breathe, reflect on what really matters in your life.

This book isn't the end of your journey, but rather the beginning of a never-ending quest for self-knowledge and personal growth, for expansion, for connection and joy. Every day is a new opportunity to discover something new about yourself, new skills, and the world around you.

Remember that life isn't about reaching a final destination, but about enjoying and learning every step of the way. So keep going, with courage and self-love, and you will allow your truth, illuminate every decision you make. Consistency, consciousness, and constant choice are the keys to a full and authentic life. May this be just the beginning of a journey full of discovery and transformations.

What is the greatest possibility available to you or me here that we have not yet recognized?

Don't be surprised by the general movements of your life, they are a product of resonance.

Vibrations create frequencies, and these frequencies are constantly moving; they nucleate themselves according to the type of frequency, and as you expand your consciousness, the environment will inevitably react on the same frequency you created.

Instead of getting angry, judging, or distressed, **THANK** those who drift away for no apparent reason and **WELCOME** those who come to join you in this new evolutionary stage. We all complete a cycle in the lives of others.

Flow at peace with those changes of scenery that you needed to see manifested dynamically for your greater expansion.

Veronica Alonso

One of My Favorite Lyrics

... Mr. Jones and me look into the future
Yeah, we stare at the beautiful women
"She's looking at you. I don't think so. She's looking at me."
Standing in the spotlight, I bought myself a gray guitar
When everybody loves me, I will never be lonely

I'll never be lonely
Said I'm never gonna be lonely

I wanna be a lion
Yeah, everybody wants to pass as cats
We all wanna be big, big stars, yeah
But we got different reasons for that
Believe in me, 'cause I don't believe in anything
And I, I wanna be someone to believe
To believe, to believe, yeah!

Mr. Jones and me, stumbling through the barrio
Yeah, we stare at the beautiful women
"She's perfect for you, man, there's got to be somebody for me."
I wanna be Bob Dylan
Mr. Jones wishes he was someone just a little more funky
When everybody loves you, ah son
That's just about as funky as you can be. ...

Partial lyrics from the song,
Mr. Jones by
Counting Cows
Released: December 1,1993
Written by: David Bryson and Adam Duritz

Signature Tasting

Since I love wines and I like to go to vineyards or explore different aromas, I'm giving you a wine-style feedback here.

This book is a simple but genuine approach to what I call "a lot like love." Even though I don't know you, I feel like I already love you. For being brave, for daring to pursue your own truths, with all the challenges and discomforts they entail.

So thank you first for buying the book, then for reading this far, and last but not least, for being yourself.

I hope we meet.

Tone and Style

Direct and straightforward, but warm. It feels like we're talking face-to-face, just the way I like it. Or as if I were talking to a very close friend.

Profound, yet accessible, avoiding unnecessary technicalities, while maintaining a certain scientific rigor.

Narrative and reflective, combining notes from personal stories with universal teachings.

Short and concise, without going into too much detail on each point, it gives it that passionate color of the grape.

I thought it was an excellent idea to define the mission, vision, and values of this, my first book. I believe it will give it a clear identity and help connect more with those who read it.

Mission

To provide you with tools for empowerment and awareness through profound truths, based on personal experience and patient stories, so you can find your own truth and transform your life.

Vision

To be a reference book on the path of self-knowledge, helping people of all ages to awaken their consciousness, strengthen their self-esteem and confidence, living with greater freedom and emotional presence in the here and now.

Value

Authenticity, clarity, and transformation. This book doesn't impose truths, but rather invites reflection and personal discovery, offering real stories, profound questions, and practical tools for inner growth.

What do you think? Would you like to join the second edition as an active participant?

My dear reader, this is more than just a literary project, it is my way of being and existing in the world.

It's about starting, initiating, launching, founding, undertaking, and projecting myself into communication outside the privacy of the consulting room where I offer everything I've learned from my life experience as well as my technical and academic training.

Don't limit yourself and dream in a big way.

See you around any corner,

With sincere love, Vero

Acknowledgments

Better dead than simple, as the saying goes, right? And to be honest, dead, no... often tired, yes.

However, here I am, with this first book in my hands, with life on my shoulders and my soul absolutely expanded. Thanks to my first analyst, who with the patience of a goldsmith and sweet kindness accompanied those initial excavations into my inner world. There, where everything was upheaved soil and dark silences, he knew how to be a lighthouse so I could dare to see. I didn't understand much, but something in me already knew that exploring inward was the only way to be reborn outward. Thanks to my sisters for the endless hours of soul-searching, talks, laughs, tears, and mutual growth. To my brother, support, mirror, shout, hug, and tribe. Thanks to the best friends I could have; who remind me that laughter is medicine for the soul. To mom, for giving me life, and for being the best grandmother.

And Dad, Rodolfo Valentino Alonso, who is no longer here, but continues to be an invitation to take courage, to start new challenges, knowing that the most powerful force is self-love and trust in my steps. To my four grandparents, and all the lineages that support my back, gifting me today the privilege of being a European citizen. My path goes back to the land from which they gave birth. And yes, I will only go back to gain momentum.

To my patients, to each one of them. Thank you for trusting, even when everything was trembling. I saw in you the hidden potentials, those we discovered word by word, silence by silence. Today, when I look at what we created together, I am not only moved but deeply proud. To the institutions, organizations, spaces, and paths that provided me with tools to make my knowledge something useful, expansive, and truly effective. Thank you to music, which always brings me back home when I get lost.

To the moments of chaos, to my insecurities, to my fears: they were not invited, yet how much they taught me. To the choices I made, even (and especially) the ones that went wrong because without them I would not have learned to create new possibilities. Thanks to my body that supported all the steps... and some falls, too. To Jesus of Nazareth, to Sigmund Freud, to Julio Bocca, Freddy Mercury, to Gary Douglas... what a combo, right? They inspired me from different stages, and from all of them I learned something about the human soul, art, madness, and expansion.

To Aunt Sara, my first role model of a woman with business, joy, and determination, when that still seemed a man's thing. To all the animals, those magical beings that taught me to coexist in diversity. I grew up on a farm, so there were many. They also have something to tell us. To love, in all its forms because it is my compass. To Gonzalo, the father of my daughter, who entrusted me without asking for the most precious thing someone can give: a life.

And finally, to our great Lulu. Thank you for life. To MY LIFE, in capital letters. To its hidden blessings, to its kindness disguised as obstacles, to its mysterious ways of helping me transcend, to my vulnerability, to the mysteries I continue to explore, to the essence of simplicity, for encouraging me to step out of polarity and separation to appreciate that everything and everyone are just doing what we came here to be. And that is a great contribution. Today more than ever, I recognize myself with permission and deep gratitude. Because when you have that – and you have yourself – you have everything.

Bibliographic References

1. "2 out of 3 ($\approx$ 2/3) of the 8 billion will die from preventable diseases."

    Noncommunicable diseases ("preventable") cause 36 million deaths per year and represent 68% of the main causes of death worldwide. Approximately 100,000 deaths per day (about 150,000 total) are related to preventable causes.

2. "13% of the world's deaths are due to heart disease, stroke, chronic respiratory diseases, cancer and diabetes."

    Cardiovascular diseases, cancer, chronic respiratory and diabetes cause the vast majority of deaths from non-communicable diseases: 7 of top 10 causes of death in 2021. This set of diseases represents approximately 68% of the 10 leading causes of death.

3. "Nearly 400 million young children suffer violence in their homes."

    Child violence is known to be high globally, according to estimates by UNICEF/WHO. According to a recent UNICEF report (June 2024), approximately 400 million children under the age of 5 – that is, 6 out of 10 in that age group – are subjected regularly to psychological aggression or physical punishment at home. Of the total, about 330 million face direct physical punishment, which involves beatings, shaking or other forms of bodily abuse by caregivers. A further breakdown details that, globally, approximately 1.6 billion children (2 out of 3), between 1 and 14 years old, experience some type of violent discipline (physical or psychological) every month.

    Expanded context: This data is based on standard surveys, such as MICS (Multiple Indicator Cluster Surveys) and DHS, which use validated methods to measure psychological aggression (shouting, insults) and physical (hitting, shaking). The WHO also reports similar figures: 6 out of 10 children under 5 years of age are victims of physical and/or psychological abuse at home, reaffirming the esteem of the 400 million.

Interpretation of the data: This number reflects "normalized" violence in homes around the world, especially in low- and middle-income countries, and has serious impacts on child development. According to the WHO, these practices:

1. lack educational effectiveness.

2. can cause trauma, mental health problems, and affect development long-term neurological system.

There are differences by region, but this phenomenon is global and persistent. In addition, 1.6 billion children (1 in 3 children under the age of 14) live under the regular disciplinary violence.

What does "regularly" mean?

When UNICEF and WHO report that "400 million young children suffer from violence regularly in their homes," it refers to a minimum monthly frequency.

This is based on the MICS (Multiple Indicator Cluster Surveys) and DHS (Demographic and Health Surveys), which measure exposure in the last four weeks. In other words, it is not an isolated event, but a repeated pattern that is part of the everyday parenting style.

What is considered domestic violence?

1. Physical punishment: spanking, hitting with objects (such as belts or canes), jerking, pushing, slapping, forcing the child to hold awkward postures for long periods.

2. Psychological aggression: shouting, insults, threats, humiliation, mockery, public or private ridicule, emotional isolation or rejection.

These practices, although some are naturalized as a discipline, are classified by international organizations as forms of child abuse. And they entail significant consequences.

Short-term impacts

• Emotional insecurity: children begin to distrust adults who should protect them.

• Low self-esteem: the implicit message is "I'm not worthy," "I deserved punishment."

• Sleep disorders, anxiety, social isolation, regressions (bedwetting, nocturnal fears).

• Problems in school performance due to concentration difficulties.

Long-term impacts

• Depression, anxiety disorders, self-harm and suicidal behaviors in adolescence and adulthood.

• Increased risk of abusive relationships (as a victim or perpetrator) when replicating models learned.

• Alterations in brain development, especially in areas such as the amygdale (emotional regulation) and the prefrontal cortex (self-control).

• Chronic physical health problems, such as hypertension, heart disease, obesity or diabetes, associated with toxic stress in childhood.

The cycle of violence

One of the most serious risks is the generational transmission of abuse. Many adults who physically punish do so because they were raised that way. And without conscience or resources, replicate what they experienced: "I was beaten and I came out well."

But the research is conclusive: punishment does not teach, it only subdues.

4. "9% of the world's population is malnourished"

In 2022, there were approximately 148 million children under the age of 5 with growth retardation (22.3%), stunting. Overall, acute malnutrition (wasting) affects 6.8% of children under the age of five years.

Global Malnutrition Indicator (FAO/UN)

The prevalence of chronic malnutrition (low sustained energy intake) in 2022 is estimated between 8.7% and 9.8%, with a midpoint of 9.2% of the world's population, equivalent to about 735 million people.

Malnutrition in children under 5 years of age: This subgroup is analyzed with data that they also provide important context:

Stunting: 148.1 million children were stunted in 2022, which corresponds to 22.3% of children under 5 years of age.

Acute malnutrition (wasting): 45 million children suffered from wasting, which represents 6.8% of those under the age of this age.

Childhood overweight: 37 million children are overweight (5.6%), a clear indication of the double burden of malnutrition.

How data interrelates: The global 9% covers both adults and children, and is based on an FAO estimate of 735 million malnourished in 2022. Of those, 148 million are retarded children and 45 million are acutely malnourished (wasting) . The difference between the general 9% and these child subgroups is explained by the fact that it also includes adults with chronic malnutrition.

Clear interpretation:

• 9% of the global population suffers from chronic malnutrition (at least 735 million people).

In children under 5 years of age, in 2022:

   • 22.3 % with stunted growth → 148 M

   • 6.8 % with acute malnutrition → 45 M

   • 5.6% overweight → 37 M

This reflects the double burden of hunger (malnutrition and overweight) and the urgency of comprehensive health and food systems.

5. "149 million 5-year-olds stunted"

In 2022, 148.1 million children under the age of 5 were affected by delayed stunting.

In 2022, there were 148.1 million children under 5 years of age stunted (stunting), equivalent to 22.3% of the global child population in this age group. This total has declined from 204.2 million in 2000

Joint Child Malnutrition Estimates 2023 (UNICEF WHO Banco Mundial): 148.1 million children (stunted) in 2022, with 22.3% global prevalence.

UNICEF Data: confirmation of number and percentage, and regional distribution (Americas) of South Africa, Sub-Saharan Africa and Asia).

WHO GHO (2024): complements with an estimated model of 150.2 million in 2024 and prevalence of 23.2%.

Current context and trends: The global prevalence fell from 33% (2000) to *22.3% (2022)*.

In 2024, the UN estimates 150.2 million, with a prevalence of 23.2%, a slight increase. The most affected regions are: South Asia and Sub-Saharan Africa, accounting for 80% of cases

> • Exact fact: "148.1 million children under the age of five were affected by stunting in 2022 (22.3%)" — UNICEF/WHO/World Bank 2023.
>
> • Data from 2000–2022 shows a reduction from 204 M to 148 M, but progress slows down.
>
> • Recent WHO 2024 figures: 150.2 M affected, prevalence 23.2%.
>
> • Almost 40% of cases in South Asia and another 40% in sub-Saharan Africa.
>
> • Only one-third of countries are on track to achieve the SDG22 target by 2030.

6. "It is estimated that 582 million will live with chronic malnutrition in the coming years"

The Gates Foundation projections indicate that there will be 40 million more children with Climate Change Delay by 2050.

"The SOFI 2024 report warns that if we do not change course, 582 million people will remain chronically undernourished in 2030, a setback to the level of 2015, just when the SDGs were launched. Africa will bear the brunt, concentrating half of the world's that figure. We are stuck, battered by conflict, climate crisis, and economies that exclude millions from access to a decent diet."

Projection: 582 million people with chronic malnutrition by 2030

Key Stats: According to the SOFI 2024 report by FAO and other UN agencies, if trends persist, around 582 million people will be chronically undernourished by 2030, with about half living in Africa. In 2023 there were between 713 and 757 million undernourished people (733 M on average), which represents 1 in 11 people in the world; Africa had a prevalence of 20.4%.

Context and trends: The increase is driven by conflict, climate shocks, economic shocks and the COVID19 pandemic, which reversed progress and stalled goals towards 2030. In 2022, more than 2.8 billion people (~35%) were unable to afford a diet. This percentage rises to 71.5% in low-income countries.

Data integration:

• Comparison: 733 M in 2023 vs. 582 M projected in 2030, revealing stagnation in the fight against hunger.

• 50% of the undernourished will be in Africa by 2030, with a focus on regional disparities.

• Multiple structural factors: wars, climate crises, poverty and inequality.

Food:

• Connection between these figures and global targets (SDG 2) and urgency in the efficient and coordinated financing, as demanded by the organizations.

7. "1 in 3 women is a victim of physical or sexual violence at some point"

According to the WHO, approximately 30-35% of women have experienced physical or sexual violence in her life. This represents about

736 million women.

8. "On average, men have a higher mortality rate and expectation of life (60 for men and 85 for women)"

Higher mortality in men: A global analysis of the Global Burden of Disease 2021 found that, for 2021, rates of mortality for men aged 15-39 years are 65.9% higher than for women aged 15-39 years. This gap persists and widens at older ages. Causes include behavioral risks (accidents, violence, suicide), diseases and less attachment to health.

Life expectancy by sex

Parameter	Men	Women	Approx. Dif
Global (births ~2020)	~70.4 years	~74.9 years	+4.5 years
Global (2021, GBD)	—		4.5 years
High Countries	~78.1 years	~83.4 years	+5.2 years
Netherlands	~61.6 years	~65.4 years	+3.8 years
USA (2023)	75.8 years	81.1 years	+5.3 years

In global contexts, the gender gap in life expectancy is around 44/45 years since 2016.

In high-income countries, the difference can be as high as 56 years.

Disparities are narrowing in low-income countries. The actual figures are:

Men: ~70 years old globally, 76/78 in rich countries.

Women: ~75 years old globally, 81/83 years old in developed countries.

Causes of these differences:

1. Biological: Men have a lower immune response, more testosterone (cardiovascular risk). Women have extra protection from estrogen.

2. Behavioral: Greater exposure of men to risks: accidents, violence, suicide. More alcohol, tobacco, and drug use.

3. Social: Men often avoid medical care, delay diagnoses and

treatments.

Solid data shows that men live about 45 years less than women.

The US (75.8 vs. 81.1), rich countries (+5 years), global inequality according to income.

Global estimates indicate a life expectancy of 68 years for men and women. 72.2 for women; in more developed countries, men 76.6 and women 82.8.

9. "In America, for the first time in this century, life expectancy decreases drastically"

It is true that "in America," especially in the US, life expectancy has suffered a sharp and unprecedented fall in most of this century, driven mainly due to COVID19, but also due to chronic diseases and deaths due to overdose.

This is the first time in this century that such a drastic and sustained decline has been seen. If you want to explore more causes or data by country/region, I'll be happy to help.

About the Author

Veronica is a psychologist and psychoanalyst, a former dancer, and the mother of a teenager with Down syndrome.

VERONICA ALONSO

Born in Buenos Aires and currently based in Florida, USA, she practices online, using a unique integrative technique that has attracted clients from all over the world.

She has worked in complex areas of clinical psychology, such as emergency medicine, social risk, and terminal illnesses. She began her career working with children, but the birth of her daughter marked a turning point: since then, she has dedicated herself exclusively to working with adults.

Throughout her career, she has addressed topics such as grief, phobias, and gender issues, and, above all, has empowered people to transform anxiety into a vital force, rather than an obstacle. Since 2019, she has incorporated energetic tools such as "Consciousness Access Bars," which promote healing processes and accelerate dynamic changes in the lives of those who consult her.

In 2024 she was a finalist in the Mujeres Transformadoras Argentina Program, promoted by Disco and Voces Vitales Cono Sur, a training and mentoring program that recognizes leading women with impactful projects. She was selected among the 20 finalists in the country for her innovative approach to mental health and therapeutic support.

Her inclusive vision and passion for well-being led her to achieve a Guinness World Record in March 2025 as part of the official Growing for Inclusion team, participating in a 24-hour tandem sports challenge alongside a blind Paralympic athlete. Today, she is part of the foundation as director of the Stimulation, Rehabilitation, Family Support, and Academic Training department.

Veronica invites people to know what they know, to reconnect with their truth, and to expand their lives to their fullest potential. Going through this counseling is not just therapy – it is a true wellness experience. Please email me at metodowellness25@gmail.com if you would like to discover more.